BY MILLEN BRAND

Poetry

Dry Summer in Provence
Local Lives
Peace March

Novels

The Outward Room
The Heroes
Albert Sears
Some Love, Some Hunger
Savage Sleep

Text for

Fields of Peace, photographs by George Tice

Screenplay

The Snake Pit (with Frank Partos)

Peace March

Millen Brand

PEACE MARCH

NAGASAKI TO HIROSHIMA

MILLEN BRAND

The Countryman Press
Woodstock, Vermont

Library of Congress Cataloging in Publication Data

Brand, Millen, 1906-1980
  Peace march, Nagasaki to Hiroshima.

  1. Brand, Millen, 1906-1980--Journeys--Japan--
Kyushu. 2. Kyushu--Description and travel.
3. Authors, American--20th century--Biography.
4. Nagasaki--Bombardment, 1945--Anniversaries,
etc.--Poetry. 5. Hiroshima--Bombardment, 1945--
Anniversaries, etc.--Poetry. 6. Peace--Poetry.
I. Title.
PS3503.R2576Z474   811'.52   80-15572
ISBN 0-914378-64-3
ISBN 0-914378-63-5 (pbk.)

First published 1980

by THE COUNTRYMAN PRESS INC.

Woodstock, Vermont 05091

For Yoshiko Miyano and Kiyo Matsufuji,
for the monks and nuns, particularly
Gyotsu Sato, Mamoru Kato, and Hideo Morioka,
for Yoshie and Ko Tentaku,
and for the children
with love.

Brief note on pronunciation

The Japanese do not accent the penultimate syllable. A three-syllable name is usually accented on the first syllable, very lightly, so Yo'shiko. In general, distribute the accent evenly over all the syllables. All vowels are pronounced separately. "E" is pronounced like long "a," so Hideo is Hid'day-oh. "G" is always hard.

The people of Hiroshima ask nothing of the world except that we be allowed to offer ourselves as an exhibit for peace. We ask only that enough people know what happened here and how it happened and why it happened, and that they work hard to see that it never happens again.

SHINZO HAMAI, *Mayor of Hiroshima,* 1949

I think that now is the time for us, survivors of the devastation of a nuclear weapon, to perform our duty for the realization of world peace by strongly advocating to all the people that not only nuclear weapons but war itself should be terminated for the sake of the future existence of humanity.

YOSHITAKE MOROTANI, *Mayor of Nagasaki,* 1975

Japan

Japan, Basho's
The Narrow Road Through the Provinces,
Oku no Hosomichi. Basho
yielding to the wind
"like a loosened cloud,"
taking his way along the coast.
Kyushu
with its roll of haiku
sounding, a faintness immortal
over the hills,
over golden shrines looking out
on pine groves.
Honshu saying
from watery panels of green reflecting
"vestiges of dream,"
Come.
        March.

June 20, 1977.   Last Year, This Year

1

Along Thirty-fourth Street in New York,
in the wide, dove-shadowed street,
a procession.
First a streamer that says
                    BOSTON TO WASHINGTON
                    WALK FOR DISARMAMENT
                              &
                         SOCIAL JUSTICE
Jim Peck has one end, I the other.
Behind us a group of Japanese
skull-shaven monks and nuns
in saffron or rust-colored robes
classically rippling at their strong
ankles and in their hands
fan drums. Mamoru Kato
meditative in his drum-protected quiet.
Beside him, Masatochi Shibuya
with his thin form, a patient organizer.
Then Hideo Morioka, a sane saint,
and Yoshiko Miyano, a poet (not a nun),
her heavy black hair falling
on her forehead. Others as well,
all walking
with the long line of Americans
eastward to the United Nations.
Their chant is a prolonged cymbal,
"Namu myo ho ren ge kyo,"
the "kyo" little more than "ko,"
repetitive syllables with their drum
accompaniment. The fan drum is a disk
of reverberent stretched membrane like a fan
held in the left hand,
the stick in the right hand

hitting hard. After every fifth beat,
a ruffle. On and on.
      "The people of Hiroshima
ask nothing of the world . . . "

2

Last year, in both New York and Washington,
I walked with these monks and nuns and Yoshiko.
They were from the Japan Buddha Sangha.
In all, sixteen Japanese
were in the American
Continental Walk for Disarmament
and Social Justice. Some walked
from San Francisco to Washington,
some on "feeder walks"
from New Orleans, Boston, other cities, coming
from the A-bombed country to be
here with us for peace.

3

This year
in memory/recognition of that
companionship sealed
in eight thousand miles of walking here,
the Sangha is asking Americans
to come and be their guests
in the Japanese annual Peace March
from Tokyo to Hiroshima.
      I read the invitation
in the War Resisters League bulletin
and phoned Jim Peck.
As I half expected, he told me
he was going. I told him
I was much tempted to go.
He said, "I hope you do."

Decision

I soon decided.
The pull of Japan,
that sun-flag country, the pull
of a wanted possibility. More than that
it was the meaning, for me, of a peace march.
        In my childhood
I was not a fighter. I had an innate dislike,
which continued as a leaven in me,
though it was hazardous not to fight.
        In my thirties
on Crow Hill in Pennsylvania
I learned the peace sects,
Mennonites, Moravians, Schwenkfelders,
their principled refusal of war. Yet war
caught me, the Hitlerian horror.
In 1943
I went to Washington and did war-service
in the Office of Civilian Defense. I even
worked later on a torpedo bomber
in the Consolidated-Vultee plant near me
in Allentown. Then the war in Europe ended
and I stopped war work.
In 1945
I was teaching in a summer conference
at the University of New Hampshire
when, in early August, a newspaper headline
appeared saying an atomic bomb
had been dropped on Hiroshima.
I thought it must be a student hoax, a put-on.
It was not. Hiroshima, that flat delta
of human life,
was ashes, a radio-active waste.
Nagasaki was added to Hiroshima,
and my childhood feelings, my leaven,

rose warm around these cities.
For force, violence
       for me
had become unworkable.
Some power other than armed force
was all that was humanly
tolerable now.
       With that conviction
I would put my aging body
on the roads of Japan.

Shoes

Soon after my decision
I went up to my son Daniel's
in Concord, Massachusetts,
and, to ready me for marching,
he bought hiking shoes, heavy, tied
with gold-thread laces like Roman
cothurni.
        I had heard
that the daily march stint in Japan
would be twenty-five to thirty kilometers.
For practice
I walked around Walden Pond,
in the northwest corner passing
the site of Thoreau's cabin—later moved
on rollers two miles uphill
and made a grain bin. I thought of the quiet
when he came down to this water
and watched its surface.
"It is a clear and deep green well . . .
a mile and three quarters in circumference."
I traveled its circuit many times
until my shoes became pliable
and I developed an airy step. Then
I took this step to my son's
summer place in the wooded valley
under New Hampshire's Mount Monadnock.
Facing its bare stone, alone
early one morning
I followed a woods road. The road
had an Indian rumor, a hint
of possible encampments.
I passed the stone-wall ends
of long-abandoned fields, the only human presence
until I came to a house

14

that unexpectedly
had a wide lawn and on it—
covered with pink, orange, and white scarves of canvas—
a pavilion
like a preview of Japan.
Its brightness in the sun
went with me back into the woods. There
in wood-edge darkness,
in pine and oak cover
but with an occasional buttercup,
with Emerson, Thoreau, and my shoes
I paid my local dues.

June 30/July 1.   Jim

We board the plane in Los Angeles
and it lifts into the dark toward the quick dawn.
        At Honolulu,
an hour's stop. From the airport railing Jim Peck
shows me Diamond Head,
a mountain at the end of mountains
hung with perpetual thunderheads.
"The clouds," he says,
nodding at their great foreheads,
"they never move.
Just stay there on
the whole row of mountains. In some places
it rains all the time and produces
rain forests. Nobody can live there."
        He has reason to be familiar with these clouds.
In 1958
he was one of the five crew members
on the ketch *Golden Rule* on its second attempt
to sail from Honolulu to Eniwetok
and block American A-bomb testing.
The Coast Guard stopped the ketch
and arrested the crew, and he spent sixty days
in a Honolulu jail. "Wearisome.
It helped me, seeing those clouds there
that never moved, just stayed there.
In the morning it was specially beautiful,
the sun coming up on them at dawn."
The sun strikes his own face,
gaunt.
        In jail, eating a dessert jelly
whose portions all the prisoners
spooned out with their own spoons,
from the mixed saliva
he contracted tuberculosis.

16

During his long stay recuperating
in St. Joseph's Hospital in New York,
I visited him.
He had a crucifix over his bed,
        atheist Jim,
and would say, "Did religion
stop World War Two?
Wars will stop when men refuse to fight."
        I wrote a preface for his first book,
We Who Would Not Kill.
And in 1961
when I was living in the south of France,
I read in an American paper,
        appalled,
that Jim, on a "freedom ride" on an integrated bus,
at the bus station in Birmingham, Alabama,
was dragged into an alley
and beaten with chains, clubs, and iron rods
until he had to have
fifty-three stitches taken in his scalp and face.
        He recovered. He continued
going his dissident, considered way
in spite of, up to now,
forty-five arrests, some illegal—
he was arrested illegally four times
on the Continental Walk—
but many times for legitimate
civil disobedience. It occurs to me
that the author of *Civil Disobedience*
spent one night in jail. Jim
persisted.

From Tu Fu, Year 759

"Army bugles are heard from every city wall;
When will it end, this loud unhappy music"

July 1.   *Fujii*

Twenty-seven Americans,
volunteers for the Peace March,
are on the plane, and more
will be arriving later.
      The Sangha, our host,
actively pursues peace. Its leader,
Nichidatsu Fujii,
a man of ninety-two, has said,
"Buddhism embodies the idea of nonviolence
in its most complete form." In 1933
he visited Gandhi at Wardha
and as they talked,
Gandhi took Fujii's fan drum and beat it,
calling it "a powerful thing" signifying
ahimsa, nonviolence. The drum
united feet and pulse in the conviction
of peace. Already then
Fujii and his followers
were building peace pagodas, stupas,
blazing white hemispheres on hills
in Japan, India, Sri Lanka,
to remind people of peace.

July 2.   The Temple

1
We arrive at noon July 2
in Tokyo, having lost a day
at the International Date Line.
Monks and nuns greet us, chanting and drumming, bowing,
and drive us down ideogram-bordered avenues
with steel overwalks at many intersections,
people on them sashed with sun.
To our right,
the imperial moat, dull.
The sky is blurred where the horizon
dies over Ueno.
        The Sangha temple
is in crowded Shibuya
at 7/8 Shinsen, a street-end.
It has ordinary
building facades, an outside stairway
up to a bed-loft, a red-girdered
middle structure, unfinished, canvas-covered,
but welcoming.
        We dump our sleeping bags and luggage
under the girders and at a small door
for the first time take off our shoes.
        A ledge for our shoes.
Going in, we touch cautious feet
to *tatami*, the reed-covered mats
that floor Japan. They feel good.
We follow this flooring
down a corridor to a large rear room
triple-altared in an elaborate clutter;
seated (lotus-position) Buddha figures,
cushions, Buddhist texts,
symbolic food (including Ritz crackers),
flowers, candles, a gong

20

to mark intervals of ritual,
a big drum, big drumstick,
and a chandelier of fluted gold.
       Around the walls are photographs
of the Sangha's peace pagodas.

2
These pagodas were built
with devout personal work. Fujii,
in building his first stupa in Japan
at Mount Hanaoka with four or five disciples,
himself wielded a pickax.
With almost no money
he and his helpers used broken shovels
and a wheelbarrow improvised
from pieces of wood lying around.
It took eight years' barefoot work,
1946 to 1954,
to build the first hemisphere,
but, when finished, it was magnificent.
Spontaneously it was felt to be
a place for encouraging peace
not just in Japan "but in the whole world."
The first World Conference of Pacifists
had been held at Gandhi's Wardha ashram.
The second was held at the just-finished
Mount Hanaoka peace pagoda.
Its photograph is here
among the others on the temple walls.

3
The altars now are moved back—
it is past noon—
and laid-down low tables
are spread for lunch. The hungry Americans
laughing together seat themselves on pads

at the table, elbow to elbow,
chopsticks in hand
(even if they cannot use chopsticks).
They are aware of the temple
as a place to live, a generous
place to sleep, eat, and spend time in.
And talk and laugh.
Their laughter
blends with the pre-meal blessing chant—
Namu myo ho ren ge kyo—
and all eat.

July 2.   The Assignment

Gyotsu Sato
eats with us, the temple's
presiding monk, a former officer
in the Emperor's army,
> a tradition in Japan,
> the changing from (defeated) military
> to moral force.
A tall man, he is accomplished in English
and talks with the *Amerikano*—
> no plural in Japanese—
across the unhurried lunch.
> Lunch finished,
he takes Jim Peck aside and says,
"I have something important to ask you.
The main Peace March
from here to Hiroshima
is halfway there, already near Osaka.
Most Americans will go on this march
though some
will go on feeder marches like one
from Tottori.
Another march—this is the important thing—
is from Nagasaki to Hiroshima.
It starts tomorrow. It needs two Americans.
They're asking you to go.
You were on the *Golden Rule*"—that means much
in Japan, marking Jim
as notable to the Japanese, particularly
because twenty-three Japanese fishermen
were irradiated and one died
in the Bikini bomb test.
"Your going will help the Nagasaki walk.
If you agree to go,
choose another American

to go with you. A train leaves at five o'clock.
I must have your answer soon."
　　　Jim speaks with me. Our intention
had been to go on the "main march"
with the other Americans,
but there are advantages to this assignment;
it would include both the bombed cities
and would be a complete march.
　　　An hour later he says,
"I have to go. Sato insists
I've got to do it to help. I've agreed." So,
I'm coming too?
　　　I ought to answer automatically.
Since his wife Paula's death,
he's been lonely and I'm the only one here
close to him. Still, for just a moment
I hesitate. It's his temperament,
how he may be if I'm the only
other American with him.
He can get angry, can be dogmatic.
Like not a few in the movement
he can be intransigent.
And might this side of his temperament
be hard to take? Still,
he has practicality,
he has a sense of humor, he has
incorruptible honesty—
the honesty of his courage—
and in any situation he lasts,
nothing puts him off. His devotion
to civil rights, to peace,
is like Fujii's, though nonreligious.
Nothing symbolic or mystic
influences him, Fujii
will not drum his way to Jim's heart, but Jim
will march with monks and nuns, with anyone
who is for peace.
　　　I tell him I'll go.

24

July 2/3.   *Night Ride*

At five we are on the train
in a night compartment
on a corridor lined with large windows;
our compartment too has windows,
and, unlike train windows in America,
these are fresh-washed, are
an invitation to look out,
framed apertures
through which, in continual changing detail,
the country we have come to
will come to us.
        Even,
on the corridor side of the train,
pullout seats like French theaters'
strapontins, aisle seats.
The train shaking along
dislodges one or two, revealing them
with a loud clack. Though they are backless,
we gladly use them for the view
of the second side of our journey,
the ocean side.
        At first on both sides,
industry, the recessed rows
of factories, the smudge
of oil and gas tanks, chimneys, struts.
Abutments of undifferentiated walls.
Advertising signs, often
a row of separate large white squares,
one for each ideogram. It's tiring,
constantly wanting Roman letters
and finding only works of art.
        Now
rice begins, bordering factories,
a pale but intense green that never varies

because the plants grow in water.
As the train rumbles into the country,
plains and plateaus of rice.
Stairs of rice on the hills.
When the train slows down,
we can see the surface of water bright
between the long rows,
but at the least change of vision-angle, water
disappears into the green.
At times a smaller field of large-leaved
lotus. Among fields
are paths, roads, and houses, farmhouses
with thatched roofs, oftener roofs
with tiles reaching down to the eaves
that blossom into endpieces
like eyes looking into space.
The commonest tile color is blue,
a shining blue. The older-building roofs
gleam with a speckled gray and gold
and sometimes red.
            Houses cluster into villages.
In a village a house will lift
a single room above the larger ground floor,
a turret, a fort-like
reminder of the samurai.
            Everywhere
the clothes of overpopulation
hang out to dry. In towns, high-rise apartments
display bright-colored dresses and drawers
on every balcony. And plastic holders
of clothes-pinned baby clothes swing out
like bird cages trying
to catch the sun. It is still the rainy season.
            Flights of rain
flick on the train windows. Too soon
night falls. The main illumination now
comes from station lights, where the names
are in both Japanese and English.

26

We find we cannot put out
our overhead compartment light.
The regimented Japanese
stay up until the lights are turned off
throughout the train, but we, exhausted
from our night plane ride, lie down,
pillowed on sleeping bags,
and rest until our beds are made.
Soon after, the train is darkened,
and the track's long drum-note ticks us south.
Jim, whose sleeping pill is alcohol,
lulled by the train's rhythm, which he likes,
sleeps deep. In the morning
we waken to a sense of sea.
During the night we tunneled unobserving
under the Strait of Shimonoseki and are now
in Kyushu—the island south of Honshu—
which we will walk across. Here again
factories, but green country too and more humid
cataracts of cloud on the mountains
that ascend from the train tracks.
Pines with vagrant arms, paths
winding upward in waterfalls of time
and mist, a likeness of classic
Japanese prints that always before
had seemed stylized. Now they are real.
        We go on,
slowed by unknown delays
in bamboo thickets, and arrive past noon—
through a crown of diluted smoke—
in Nagasaki. At the train door
our new hosts bow deep and beckon.
        Hurry! The train is late.
        The march is waiting.

July 3.   *Peace Park, Nagasaki*

1

We go by car
to Peace Park where the marchers wait
in the hot sun, with parasols out
like private canopies.
Women in below-the-knee skirts
stand by men in Sunday suits,
a drawn-up regiment headed
by a boy holding a banner
almost too big for him.

2

Peace Park is on a hill
and its focus—all the marchers face it—
is "the Peace Statue":
a statue thirty feet high that "can be seen
far off" like Fujii's peace pagodas.
"A sculptor named Seibo Kitamura
made it. He was born—just here—
in Nagasaki Prefecture." The statue,
a seated bronze man draped
with a robe over one arm
and over his loins, has
a calm Buddha look.
His raised right arm
"points to the sky
from which dropped the A-bomb,"
and his left arm with the robe over it
is stretched out "demanding peace."
From him the park slopes down
to an avenue paralleling
the Urakami River
along which we are going to march.

28

3

We begin being introduced.
Michio Aoyama will be our captain
for the first of five prefectures (states),
a young man thin and quick-moving, with the bearing
of one who goodhumoredly penetrates
into life. He works
on a research ship
for the Japan Meteorological Agency
and wears a yellow sweatshirt.
Our interpreter,
Toshi Tokuhisa, is a serious
fourth-year college student.
        Aoyama can also speak some English
and shows us, below,
a tall stone post, "There," that marks
the center of the A-bomb's explosion,
"the hypocenter." Around it
no buildings, only green foliage
that has replaced the devastation. Further south
is the International Cultural Hall, housing
a museum of the bombing. As I stand here this short distance
from the hypocenter post
looking up at a now-empty sky,
I cannot help thinking of *Bock's Car,*
the B-29 that dropped the bomb,
and imagining myself under it.

4

There have been speeches in Japanese
and TV cameramen and newspaper photographers—
the march start
is a media event. Jim
is asked to make a speech.
He has had the forethought back in New York
to write a speech and have a friend,
Yukio Aki,

translate it into phonetic Japanese.
"I am happy
to be one of the Continental Walkers
here in Japan
to bring a message of solidarity
from the American people.
No more Hiroshimas!
No more Nagasakis!
I am sorry I cannot speak Japanese.
I have had these few words translated
so that I can better convey to you
how deeply we feel on this issue."
　　　　The two lines, "No more Hiroshimas!
No more Nagasakis!" are in English:
he has been told that all Japanese
know them. Several near us
say they understand all he has said
and thank us, Jim and me, for being here.

July 3.   The Start of the March

Banners are lifted and waved,
parasols folded. Two men in front hold
a white march-identifying streamer
behind which Jim and I are asked to walk.
We start, we pass the hypocenter post,
the dark shaft of the city's sorrow,
pass the Urakami Railroad Station,
Nagasaki's main station, pass
many bright building fronts. Above one building
flies a dark-metal
copy of an origami bird.
An impression everywhere of newness.
Energy. I feel the quickening unison
of the march, a subdued elation
in the sun that now is tempered
by slightly saline-smelling air
from the water. At main street intersections,
pedestrian bridges, as in Tokyo
with many hundreds crossing.
I mention to our interpreter,
Tokuhisa,
how useful the bridges must be.
        "Yes," he says,
"but there are some complaints about them
from old people and people in wheelchairs."
        We talk. He is studying economics,
learning English
with the thought of going abroad
"to develop foreign trade."
His voice merges with other voices,
with the sound of steps refracted
from new facades.
        This newness, this forcible
rush of energy. It seems

as if rebuilt Nagasaki
rejects its hurt, wants to restore
the shape—even the beauty—of the past
in this centuries-old
tipped mountain-basin harbor pouring itself
out to sea. From 1588 on,
it was the one harbor authorized
for the Portuguese and Dutch. Tokuhisa
tells me a story about that time—
"the twenty-six martyrs." When the Portuguese
were here trading, they began to make
Christian converts. The feudal ruler
Hideyoshi considered this threatening
to the realm, a subversion,
and decreed being Christian a crime.
All who were suspected
were asked to walk across a floor
on which was painted a figure of Mary.
If they avoided stepping on it,
they were identified as Christian.
Twenty-six were given the privilege
of dying as their god had died.
       Aoyama stops the procession
to rest in a small streetside park.
       Urinals. In Japan as I will learn
       there is little privacy
       to this natural function. Here
       just an open door and troughs.
Again marching. I see posters
of men and women candidates for office,
one resembling Marcel Marceau
with Marceau's ravaged smile. On past
the Mamachi Shopping Center,
then the Suwa Shrine,
and at last, near a stream named
the Nakashima ("Mid-stream Island"),
on the city's southern outskirts,
we reach our afternoon's

goal, a large Shinto shrine.
The shrine has *torii*—wooden gates—
and a flight of steps. Tired,
we stretch out on the steps. Jim,
arms spread, with his eyes closing, says,
"Well, we've started."

July 3.   The Paper Cranes

At the shrine,
as we rest, I notice on a marcher
a necklace of threaded origami birds
like the bird
on the building we passed. I ask about it.
Through Tokuhisa:
         The necklace
is paper cranes. A paper crane—
he gives me one, do I know about it?
         No—
is for health. The crane
according to Japanese legend
lives a thousand years, so a paper crane
means a wish
for a happy, long life.
Ten years after the atom-bombing
a twelve-year-old girl in Hiroshima,
Sadako Sasaki, who had been exposed
to the bomb's radiation,
developed leukemia. A friend
sent her a letter in the hospital,
enclosing a paper crane.
Sadako thought,
If I fold a thousand cranes,
I have to get well. She folded
nine hundred and sixty-four and died.
         After she died, her classmates
at Nobori-cho Elementary School
wanted a statue for her,
to be as well
for all bombed children who died.
Newspapers took it up,
funds were raised all over the country,
and the statue was put up

in Hiroshima's Peace Park,
for there is a Peace Park there also.
Sadako now in bronze
holds over her head
the outline of the paper crane,
and there are always thousands of offered
paper cranes at the foot of her statue,
which has written on it,
"This is our cry, this is our prayer—
to make peace in the world."

July 3/4.   *Mayor Morotani*

1
Darkness in Nagasaki now, except for the lights
on Mount Inasa, and quiet, except for the silk rustle
of the Nakashima stream running
under our window.
          A rope hangs beside the window
          to lower yourself with
          in case of fire. Fire. We sleep well
          in the unburning city.
In the morning, waking,
we go down to the hotel lobby.
The march
is to leave without us on its first lap
to Isahaya.
There are other plans for us today,
march-connected and peace-connected.
          As we wait, I happen to glance
at the lobby television—TV
is everywhere in Japan. The program
is a newscast,
the Peace Statue with its Buddha calm
and the camera moving down to Jim
making his speech to the marchers.
Next a shot of Jim and me walking,
both of us frowning in sunlight,
and the panning camera then
viewing the whole line of march,
the banners, the blocks-long unison.
A clerk in the hotel lobby
turns the TV to another newscast: us again.
And our today's host, when he comes, shows us
our pictures in five newspapers.
"I guess," Jim says to me privately,
"they're getting leverage out of us.

36

It's okay." More leverage: we're being taken
to see the mayor of Nagasaki.

2

We have with us a new interpreter,
Yoshio Sekiguchi,
from Kagoshima. He tells a story
about his city. Once, as it prospered,
the Shogunate sent spies to watch it,
and the people invented their own language
to confuse the spies.
Now, Sekiguchi says,
many still talk this language. "Sometimes
I have trouble understanding them."

3

When we enter the mayor's office,
we find five reporters there
and a news photographer.
The mayor, Yoshitake Morotani,
has sharp black eyes. After the introductions
he asks Jim and me the always
first question in Japan:
"How old are you?" Jim tells him
he is sixty-two. I say, "Seventy-one,"
and tell him I am a writer.
The Mayor says, "I paint
but not very well."
       He gives us both a packet of material—
especially put together for us—
on the A-bombing. Later
I read what he said two years ago:
"Peace is generated within the human heart,"
and, "When all the people of the world
really recognize and understand
the sorrow and anguish" of the two A-bombings,

there may be "a wave,"
causing another larger wave that will develop
"into a world-encompassing peace movement."
He has been energetic,
unremittingly hopeful. He signs for us
the 1977
appeal against the bomb
from "Representative Personalities in Japan."
Jim tells him
that on the Continental Walk last year
they gave copies of this appeal in English
to mayors along the way. He says,
"Some showed sympathy,
especially the mayor of New Haven
where Yale is." Mayor Morotani
listens with interest. He has
the color of passion in his eyes.
　　　　He is given a white silk ribbon
　　　　on which to write a greeting to the march.
　　　　He asks for his brush and inkstone
　　　　and inscribes
　　　　a series of black characters
　　　　like action art.
The news photographer wishes a picture
of the mayor posed with us
in front of a small replica
of the Peace Statue. The mayor, standing,
comes just up to my shoulder and Jim's.
When we leave (I have learned manners),
I bow deeply.

July 4.   Further in City Hall

1
In the City Hall
we are taken to see Hideo Yokoo,
Chairman of the Municipal Assembly.
He urges us somewhat formally
to "do your best for peace in the United States
as I do here."
We go to the union offices—
in Japan the city employee unions
are usually in the city hall.
We call on Kazutoshi Akitake,
Chairman of the High School Teachers' Union.
He sits behind a book-piled desk,
a stream of light coming in windows
like a welcome. We sit around him
in this light.
          We ask if high-school students
are taught about the bombing. He says
there is a tendency
to want to forget, there is a tendency
in the national government
to want to minimize accounts of the bombings
in textbooks. His belief, his union's belief
is that the memory should be kept alive.
There is at present a prefectural project
to publish *In the Sky Over Nagasaki,*
An A-bomb Reader for Children. The book's preface:
"It is very difficult for your teachers
to explain the horror of the atomic bomb
to all of you who have not experienced war.
Why do they want to teach you about war
and the atomic bomb? It is because they want you
to be well aware of the horror of war,
so that you will forever protect peace."

The book is presumably told
by a hundreds-of-years-old camphor tree
just outside the Sanno Shrine.
All its leaves and limbs were blown off
in the bombing, but it survived.
Here is a passage, the tree speaking:
        "I was told that the worst place
was at the edge of the Urakami River.
Under the Ohashi Bridge
an uncountable number of people
had fallen dead on top of one another.
Some were covered with water.
Others floated on the water . . .
It was like a scene from hell."
        At the end of the book,
the most terrible story. A boy,
Fumiki Nagoya, of Hiroshima,
was born fifteen years after the bomb
to which his mother had been exposed.
At first he was a chubby,
healthy-looking boy, but then
he "did not want to eat,
he had a fever all of the time,
his gums became swollen,
pus formed inside his mouth,
his face swelled up out of shape."
The symptoms were the same as those
of his mother's "A-bomb disease."
She survived. He did not.
When he was in the second grade in school,
he died.

2
Radiation, the one all-important difference
between any previous bombing
and atom-bombing. No matter how bad
"conventional" bombing was,

some escaped. None escape the atom bomb.
In Hiroshima
over three hundred thousand
were directly exposed. Were irradiated.
A hundred forty thousand died
within five months, and those remaining alive
were *hibaksha,* contaminated "victims."
All would show the sickness,
some would die early,
others would be well for years,
then take sick without warning
and die. Resistance to disease
would be less among *hibaksha.*
     In Hiroshima the bomb dropped
in the center of the city. Here
in Nagasaki it dropped at the city's edge
and the mountainous terrain gave some protection.
Seventy thousand died in five months.
     Tens of thousands more were "exposed,"
and those exposed, in both cities,
were not just those under the bomb.
The ground a half mile from the hypocenter
was left strongly radioactive
after the bombing. For a hundred hours this
residual danger was at a maximum,
and there was some danger
for two to three weeks. All those
who came to hunt for relatives and friends
to help them
were themselves irradiated and many
became ill or died.
Rescue squads, volunteers
who came in to help were irradiated. Further,
a "black rain" fell
following the detonation, a rain
dripping in sooty lines down white walls
and falling on human skin. It was hard
to clean off, it carried radiation.

In places
it contaminated water. This downpour
Masuji Ibuse
wrote about in a novel, *Black Rain,*
and the term became familiar
throughout Japan.
What was this "radiation sickness"?
In some there were immediate
and terrible symptoms.
Hair fell out, the face lost its features,
there was loss of control
of the normal body functions,
there was an agonizing thirst.
Some threw themselves into water
or drank grease-coated water,
irradiated water.
If they recovered, as many did,
they still had, in their bodies,
various radio-active particles:
it might be uranium, plutonium,
cesium, strontium—no matter how small,
these absorbed particles were hazardous
and settled down in bone marrow
or their tender tissues. The cells of their bodies
carried effects of neutrons, gamma rays,
beta rays. All these effects—aftereffects—
stayed. Months later, years later,
they might have the same symptoms
others had suffered immediately.
They might sicken suddenly and die.
So those who recovered did not know
how long their recovery would last.
More awful, more dreadful, no woman
knew what her womb would produce.
Such were the results
of the first bombs. Today
a single bomb
can do a thousand times as much damage

42

as the bombs dropped on Hiroshima
and Nagasaki. Exploded
at the right height it can devastate
and irradiate an area the size
of several prefectures.
How can sanity
and this bomb exist together?

3
Suppose those exposed to the Nagasaki
or Hiroshima bomb,
those at a saving distance,
were by luck not seriously affected,
the radiation not reaching a vital organ,
the body relatively unhurt; still
merely to be known as exposed
was to be, to a degree,
an outcast, "contaminated." Everywhere
the radiated were avoided.
Many had trouble marrying.
Many had trouble getting jobs.
If they had scars, keloids, visible evidence,
their predicament was still worse.
This does not mean that no *hibaksha* married.
Chairman Akitake of the Teachers' Union
married a *hibaksha*. One may imagine
the love he felt, but also
the concern. "We waited three years
before we had a baby. We were
very apprehensive." The child was normal,
but their fear will be lifelong.
Akitake has helped
with "the international symposium on the damage
and aftereffects of the bombing."
He knows too well what these aftereffects
are, knows the unpredictable presence, the glow
in the cells like an unending ember.

He, his wife, and other
tens of thousands for thirty-two years
have experienced this continual
torment.

July 4. There's No Trace of That Terrible Day Now

From the City Hall
we go across the city
back to Peace Park, to the International Cultural Hall,
that building we saw yesterday housing
"the Atomic Bomb Material Center." Jim and I
go through floor after floor of this building.
A not-well-organized but sufficient
record of the hour and moment, 11.02 A.M.,
when the bomb
stopped a clock, the frame
broken and two loops hanging.
On view: Shattered concrete walls.
Other buildings
reduced to crumpled steel frames like rows of tumbleweed.
All wood, ashes.
Telegraph poles as if lightning-struck, on fire.
A trolley on its side, its content
spilled out as if a hot wind
had thrown the passengers, burned naked, into a ditch.
Shadows of human beings
left permanently on walls.
A hand stuck to melted glass, the bones, the glass
in their conjunction of hypocenter heat
become a modern fossil. Stretchers, trains.
"Victims carried off the relief train,"
huddled figures beside the train
beet-red like the just-born.
Silence.
Keloid quivers.
Silence.

On one floor a poem, translated:
"I'm a boy in the fourth grade now.

At a primary School called Yamazato.
The playground is cleared up now:

"There's no trace of that terrible day now,
My playmates do not know that
Many people . . . were once burned to ashes.

"I recall casually that very day:
I crouch where Mother was burnt
And feel the earth with all fingers.

"When I dig deep with a bamboo there,
Pieces of black charcoal appear,
And Mother's face is seen deep in the earth."

Jim refuses a last floor. It is too much.
A woman near us
is in tears. She glances at us.
What are we doing, Americans
looking at this?

July 4/5.   The City

1
Leaving the too-great sadness,
we go across the city again
to the base of a hill
covered with the city's symbol, hydrangeas,
and climb to the Glover House
and, privileged Americans,
inspect, below us,
the well-reconstituted parallels
of streets and roofs. Again I think,
as I did marching yesterday,
What beauty! In the buildings,
in the city's structure,
beauty even in the harbor's
shipyards and the world's
largest derrick, its frame
like a giant robot against the shore.
At our feet, the hydrangeas'
white clusters.

2
Tonight
we stay again in our room over the Nakashima stream
and in the morning, early, are driven
to overtake the march in Isahaya.

July 5.   At Isahaya

He is waiting outside the station.
"My name is Chiyomatsu Kanagae.
I'm seventy-three years old,
so when the bomb dropped on Nagasaki,
I was forty-one." He wears
brown pants, a short-sleeved clean white shirt,
and a straw hat.
Because his sleeves are short,
he can show me his burned arm
mottled with scars like fish scales.
"The reason I got burned:
I was a locomotive engine driver
and I was at the station
about twenty-five hundred meters
from the hypocenter. At the alarm
I went to the station shelter,
but came out as the bomb exploded.
I thought the flash, the *pika,* was near,
so I did what the school children did
when they practiced. I put my hands
over my eyes and fell to the ground.
After I got up,
I could see everything burning. I saw many
caught under wreckage, children.
Both my children
were on the small island outside
Nagasaki Harbor. It's past
that giant crane. You've seen it?"
          "Yes, I've seen it."
          "So my children and wife were safe.
I'm still diseased. There is no known
cure for the A-bomb disease.
Today I feel well.
Yesterday I felt dull and ill."

He has to go twice a year
to the hospital to be examined.
He does not complain. His face,
his saved eyes are extremely quiet.
He is a man
who once lived in the engine house
"because my duty was there."

July 5.   To Omura

From Isahaya we walk all day
to Omura. Our interpreter here
overnight
is Kunio Nakajo, English teacher
"of the Omura Horticultural High School."
He was born September 29, 1924,
on Tsushima Island
off shore in the Tsushima Strait.
He goes with us to visit the mayor
with whom he talks
with a natural, instantaneous
élan vital, life leap.
      From the mayor's we walk to a nearby
outdoor meeting place, a place of seats
arranged haphazardly under arbors, yet
a theater, an agora
with a plinth of water holding
the reflection of a park.
      Jim
reads his phonetic Japanese speech
to forty or fifty listening. Then questions,
and Nakajo interpreting.
His spoken English has limits,
but his verve is limitless.
We wish we had the words
to respond more deeply to all the dark eyes
so responsibly fixed on us. We cannot.
Unless the speaking of our eyes
answers.

July 6. The Ritual of the March

Jim and I have now learned
the procedure of the march. Most
of the Japanese march only one day.
They wear any kind of shoes,
even clogs. They march steadily.
Ahead of us a sound-truck broadcasts
the purpose of the march. On its tape
I hear a constant repeating of
"Jim Peck-san" and "Millen Brando-san."
I ask a marcher what it says:
"'Jim Peck, American peace activist,
sixty-two years old,
and Millen Brand, American author,
seventy-one years old,
are walking with us.'"
            Now the truck is broadcasting a song,
            "We Shall Overcome" in English,
            the main American freedom song.
Some of the marchers carry
large collection boxes, cardboard cartons
covered with red or black ideograms,
slogans for peace.
The streamer at the head of the march
says, "The Japanese nation
is walking for peace."
            The "main banner" is a deep green;
others are red, blue, pale blue
like fragments of sky, Kenji
Myazawa's "blue night's wind."
Some banners
fly like echoes of roof tile.
From a bamboo pole cascade
thousands of paper cranes
in their flights of health and sadness.

From another pole hangs
a small but soon-to-be-larger
collection of the white ribbons
mayors have brushed greetings on.
So the long, well-bound-together
line winds north
toward the sea.
          At ten-thirty we rest.
It may just be beside the road
or it may be near a store
where we can get something to drink,
small bottles of milk, *gyunyu,*
or cans of *Kaffee Gyunyu,* coffee milk.
The rest stop is important.
We have been walking in humid heat
that pours sweat into our eyes.
Resting revives us.
          At noon, lunch; then in the afternoon,
another rest stop, where I flap out
my wet shirt-back in the shade.
          Part of the daylong march:
by appointment town by town,
city by city,
we see mayors. Sometimes
the mayor comes out to greet us, speaking
from the city-hall steps. More often
the marchers draw up, banners at attention,
and Aoyama, Jim, I, and our interpreter
and perhaps one or two others
are taken inside to a room
of invariably
leather-upholstered chairs and a low
table. The anteroom of the mayor's office.
At the proper moment the mayor appears
and all stand and bow and he says, *"Dozo"*
("Please be seated").
He sits down too.
Jim reads his now-called "message,"

and Aoyama talks with the mayor
in his good-humored young way
and asks him to sign "the appeal."
       Most sign at once.
       A few hesitate
       but cannot be "against peace."
Now the mayor is offered
one of the white silk ribbons
to inscribe like Mayor Morotani
with a greeting to the march. Before we leave,
unobtrusively
the mayor gives Aoyama
a small white folded parchment envelope
embossed with a crane flying
or with flowers, and encircled
with many tied colored strings—
a gift of money, maybe ten thousand yen.
       At one of the first of the visits
the mayor, impressed with Jim and his speech,
gave him the parchment of money.
Seeing this decoratively wrapped
packet of unknown content,
Jim thought it was a present to him
and put it in his pocket.
After we left the mayor's office,
Captain Aoyama had to tell him
that it was for the march, not for him,
and Jim, embarrassed, excusing himself, gave up
the beautiful packet.
       At five o'clock or thereabouts
the day's march ends.
We who have marched all day now
meet another group, those
who are to march tomorrow, untired,
enthusiastically lined up
awaiting us. Many
have straw hats shadowing
their shoulders, the women

modestly skirted (no miniskirts hardly
in Japan), often young people
and children, the group
giving the clear impression
of a cross section of the town.
As we come up striding,
concealing our fatigue, they cheer
and wave. Now
the ritual of meeting:
we line up facing them
and one by one
with a soft flourish of cloth in air,
with a becoming slowness,
we pass them our banners.
There are speeches: a union leader
or local peace activist talks
into a microphone with a dangling unattached
wire, or a microphone attached
to the sound truck's loudspeaker.
There is a hint of *aijo,*
affection, though the Japanese
are not demonstrative.
Friends are meeting friends.
Friends are leaving friends.
It is the end
of a good day.

July 6.   The Inn

1
This evening we go
to an old-style Japanese inn
in the town of Kawatana. "Ah ah ah,
we saw you on TV.
We know you." All the personnel watch as
at the low entrance step—
in from the eave-bordered street—
we change from shoes to slippers. New-shod,
we are guided by the mistress of the inn
up steep stairs, down a long corridor,
to an unmarked door that slides open:
a large *tatami*-mat room.
I step in with my slippers on.
Aoyama, shocked, cries,
"No, no. You must take off slippers!"
and when I have taken them off,
"Isn't it pleasant," he says,
"to have the feet . . . bare?"
He means stockinged feet. I say yes.
Jim especially likes this freedom
of trampoline reed. Aoyama
urges us to remember
where the room is, because room doors
have a deceptive likeness
and none are locked. In Japanese inns
nothing is stolen. If we open wrong doors,
possibly
a marital scene or young girls
dressing or undressing.
No chairs in the spacious room.
The low table leans against the wall.
The eighteen-mat room
is a perfect square. On a ledge

beside the sliding window-shutters
are two clean kimonos, dark blue
and imprinted with a few white lines
like footprints in snow.
          "How do you like it?"
          We turn.
In the door stands Nakajo, from Omura,
come to have dinner with us. At once
we feel his exuberance, the promise
of helpful acclimation and ease.

2

For dinner the inn mistress has returned
and pulls down the table to the floor
and seats herself at its head.
A servant girl is bringing the food. Now
Nakajo says, quite nonchalantly,
"Remove your pants."
True the room is warm,
but with women present?
He sees the direction of our glances.
"It's all right," he says. "Custom,
is the custom, to be comfortable."
And he is taking off his own pants,
meantime chatting with the mistress
in Japanese. We hesitantly
take off our pants too, since evidently
it is acceptable, not even noticed,
and we seat ourselves at the table.
I with some discomfort.
My discomfort is physical.
          I am not trained to be chairless.
          My back hurts. My legs do not know
          where to go.
          This will be my problem
          throughout the march.
The mistress attends to our wants.

We have not only food
but *sake*. Insidious, drinking *sake*,
for not you yourself
fill and refill your cup,
but another person drinking with you;
whoever notices your cup is empty,
or even half-empty, fills it.
You drink continuously then,
the prisoner of courtesy.
The mistress offers—urges on us—
each dish, each delicacy.
Soup with a green garnish. Raw fish
in pink quadrilaterals. Squid
in a dark sauce, bean-curd in a light sauce.
Foods we do not even know.
          What we do know by now
is that the appearance of food
is a high art in Japan.
Like flower arrangement, like their gardens,
every meal is thought-out, a visual
tour de force: a leaf like a green light
laid on a dark liquid, meat
carved like architecture, relish
like a modernist abstraction.
Nakajo tells us, "There is a saying,
'The Japanese eat with their eyes,
the Chinese with their mouths.'
The Chinese cook well, are even
gourmet cooks, but the Japanese
think always, How does it look?"
          We are not hurried, we eat and talk,
Jim alone
eating somewhat sparingly, as always.
But he is appreciative. The mistress
puts on the room lights,
the sun having set, and when we finish
the last course,
receives our devout thanks, bows, and leaves.

3

We are alone.
Jim brings out his whiskey bottle,
the real drink, Suntory, and, to greet it, Nakajo
teaches him the soaring word,
"Kanpai, kanpai," toasting
us and peace.
Holding his cup in one hand,
he gets to his feet
        (more comfortable, I think)
and approaches the back wall,
the smooth space beside the door
like a great blackboard. On this board
with his free hand he sketches
an imaginary map, the map of his schooling.
"Here, mathematics." From island to mainland.
"Here, English." From mainland campus to campus.
"Here, psychology." The journey of his learning
takes its immaterial place on the wall
under his moving hand.
        Jim lights
his after-dinner cigar
        (spurts of first smoke)
and Nakajo,
seated again, removes a cigarette
from his pack of Seven Stars.
All brand names of cigarettes
in Japan are in English:
Seven Stars, Hope, even Peace.
Peace . . .
We pour more drinks, but
what is Suntori without song?
Jim and I sing "We Shall Overcome,"
then all of us together sing
the song of the march,
"Genbakuo Yurusumaji,"
"Ban the Bomb." Jim and I
are just learning it and have it written—

"*Furusato no machi yakare*"—
with the translation beside it:
"My home town was burned by the A-bomb. The bones
of my relatives are buried
under the hot ground. But now
white flowers are blooming there.
May this tragedy never
happen again. No more atomic bombs
ever again in our town."
The song is invasive. It is a harmony
of reiterant melancholy
as in two of its lines:
"*Aa yurusumaji genbakuo,*
Mitabi yurusumaji genbakuo."
One line of the song has a difficult rhythm,
but we are beginning to master it,
and Nakajo helps us with it.
Then in his tenor voice
he sings, solo, "The Song of the Dolls,"
a change, a lightening
following the *Genbakuo:*
"*Sakura, sakura yayoino sorowa—*"
He says,
"This song is sung at the doll festival
in March, on the third of March.
Each family then
sings this '*Sakura.*'"
We so much like it,
we make him sing it again. "*Sakura, sakura—*"

July 7.   Toward Sasebo

We reach the outskirts of Sasebo
at lunch time and are invited
to eat in the roadside office
of the All Japan Day-Pay Workers Union.
Over his tin of food
Jim asks what the union is.
          "It's a union of day-pay workers
employed at temporary jobs they get
through the Labor-Exchange Offices.
Our national rate of unemployment
appears to be much lower
than in the United States,
under two percent, but there still are
large numbers of unemployed.
The union helps them to live."
          Jim says,
"Whom do you negotiate with?"
          "If it's the city level, as it is here,
it's the mayor. Then there's the prefectural level,
the governor, and on up. We negotiate wages.
Every year. The contract goes for a year.
All belong, a hundred in this section,
eight hundred in the city.
It's good in this area."
          Jim asks,
"Why is this union interested in peace?"
          "Oh, most unions are interested in peace."
          "In my country, no.
The peace movement gets almost no support
from unions. For instance,
we had no trade unionists
on our Continental Walk for Disarmament."
          This baffles the women and men here.
They look at one another, puzzled.

60

2
After lunch Aoyama
carries one of the banners,
one on which a dove of peace flies.
As we pass a clump of bamboo,
a live dove like a second symbol
flies across the road.

July 7.   *On the Afternoon March*

After climbing a long hill,
we have a rest period and sit beside the road.
I sit by the Vice President
of the All Japan Day-Pay Workers Union local,
an older man like me. We are silent
behind our separate languages, though
the glance between us is friendly.
There is no interpreter with us.
The VP rubs his legs, kneading
his tired muscles. I start to knead mine too,
and he shows me on his own legs:
Do it this way, get
the muscles relaxed.
He offers me a cigarette. I shake my head no.
He imitates smoking and shakes his head, meaning,
You don't smoke. I nod that he is right.
I point to the sun. A gesture of his says,
Yes, it is hot.
When we must resume marching,
he gets up first, reaches his hand to me,
and pulls me up. Again
a look between us, of friends.
We know we have had
a good conversation.

July 7.   The Burned, the Wounded

Three hours
after the bomb fell on Nagasaki
a relief train came into the city,
its smokestack issuing faintly purple smoke.
It stopped one and three-tenths kilometers
north of the hypocenter.
Tracks beyond that point were destroyed,
and the Urakami and main stations
were in ruins.
The surviving burned and wounded, those who could,
came staggering to board the train.
When it was full, some climbed
to the roof and lay there
to be carried back and out of the city.
The train and succeeding trains
took thousands to the towns, the cities
we have been walking through,
to Isahaya, to Omura, even
to Sasebo.

July 7.   Sasebo, at the Base

Sasebo with
a quarter of a million people.
A long time walking through it.
        At a street intersection, a sign,
"Maritime Self-Defense Force": Sasebo,
an East China Sea port,
is a Japanese and an American
naval base. American nuclear submarines
and the "Big E," the nuclear-powered
aircraft-carrier "Enterprise,"
once used the American naval base,
but it was reported
both here and at Yokosuka
that there was radiation "in the environment"
after their visits. Two hundred and twenty thousand
demonstrated against the "Big E,"
and thereafter, no visit.
        When we come to City Hall,
the mayor refuses to see us,
the only mayor so far who will not.
We still have
an option. Jim, I, and Aoyama
and some others
drive to a flat embankment
above a strip of water beyond which is
the American naval base. Jim
with the truck's loud-speaker volume well up,
in his raw, insistent voice—
lifetime antiEstablishment voice—
makes a speech: "Go home"
across the silent moat of water.
Who hears? And where are the photographers
who took Jim before? But back
at the News Room at City Hall

one photographer is sorry
he doesn't have a picture.
It's not too late. We take him
the long trip
back to the same embankment, the same moat,
and he photographs Jim again
trying to reach
his fellow-Americans.

July 8.   A Room Looking Toward Hirado

1

This afternoon, after the hard day's march—
sometimes so unrelievedly hot
that when a truck passes, one of those long Suzukis,
we're glad for the slight wind from it—
after the march
through Sasa and Yoshii, we end
at a modern inn near Tabira
looking across a wave-laced strait
to the island of Hirado.
      Hideko Yamaga, a pretty young
English teacher from that island,
meets me. "Your interpreter."
Meets Jim. We get acquainted,
we like her,
her sleeveless blue dress, bare arms,
her look of competence and poise.
We walk with her to a point
overlooking the strait.
      Boats
are going through as on a through highway,
and we hear their engines beating,
their warning whistles—
tugs, ketches, larger boats.
"You'll be hearing them all night,"
Miss Yamaga says.
The work clock
of night.

2

Tonight Aoyama
shares the room with us. The small *tatami* room's

cupboard
contains the three-fold mattresses
that can be spread out side by side
to the floor's end.
        Before dinner,
baths. Mandatory. Aoyama,
about to take his bath, asks us—
if the phone rings for him—
please, a message. He writes the message:
*"Ichiji kan sitara
kakete kudasai
Aoyama wa imasen."*
"After an hour
please give me a call
otherwise not here."
I know that *"kudasai"* means "please."
A marcher wrote for me,
"Sumimasenga mizu o kudasai,"
"Please give me water." On the march
I have an unquenchable thirst. Pitying
waitresses give me *"mizu"* and *"motto mizu"*
("More water"). I can't believe
the human capacity—
in highway heat—
for losing body moisture. I drink three glasses
of water and in fifteen minutes
I'm suffering again from thirst.
        The boats in the strait are drumming.
The sky over Hirado
is lined with horizon strokes of amber. Aoyama
comes back from his bath smelling faintly
of resinous soap
and, supple and young, gratuitously
touches
his hands to the floor. "No call?"
        "No call."
        While Jim is bathing,
I talk with Aoyama.

His father is an office worker. His mother
"teaches how to knit sweaters."
He has a sister in college. He says that after
his prefecture stint with us,
he must return to his "research ship"
and go to sea for a month.
Going to sea—I think, Friend Jim
has had his go at working on ships.
Aoyama's ship, the *Chofumaru,*
"two thousand sixty-six tonnage,"
is one of six. It has
twenty-two crew members
and ten research workers. He is in the group
doing research.
They take water from the sea's surface,
from ten meters down, fifty,
a hundred, two hundred,
five hundred, and if the sea is deep,
a thousand meters. They analyze
the captured water. They measure wave intervals,
wave height, water temperature, atmospheric pressure,
wind direction. Is it to protect
against Japan's tidal waves, typhoons?

3
Jim comes back, lights his cigar—
puff puff—
and sits by the window, admiring
the boats endlessly passing in the strait.
He says, "Wouldn't this be
a great place for a honeymoon?"

July 8.   *Bathing*

1

You carry your plastic basket
to an open foyer. As you take off your clothes
and drop them into the basket,
women pass, unconcerned.
        This thing of disregard
        for nudity in Japan.
You enter the bath. It has a tile floor
and a deep, sunken tub filled with water, covered
with wooden panels to keep the heat in.
You remove the panels. Heavy steam
rises from the water. You don't get in
but take dipperfuls of the water
and pour them over yourself
and soap and rinse with more water
that runs to a drain in the floor.
Only now, completely clean,
since others will use the bath water,
do you get into the tub. Deep in it
is a small ledge to sit on. Seated there
you're in water up to your chin.
Now to soak. The danger is parboiling.
Your skin may turn red.
You may get faint. You may even have
heart-failure.
        Seeing
how rapidly I come back from the bath,
the Japanese
do not believe I appreciate properly
the privilege of hot water.

2

The first time Jim took a bath, uninstructed,

he soaped and rinsed off in the tub.
Ai ai.
The water had to be drained out.
The tub had to be cleaned.
The water had to be reheated. It was
a crisis
       and lesson to me.
Japanese abroad, I learn later,
have the opposite problem.
Not instructed in western bathing,
they fill the tub with hot water
and soap and rinse themselves on the floor.

July 8.   *One Result of the Heat*

I've been carrying a notebook
in my shirt pocket, Basho business
on our hot narrow road through the prefectures,
its memoranda meant
to help me with my journal.
          Yesterday
I wanted to make a note and found the book
drenched, sweat running the ink
like a spilled glaze down the pages
and the pages clinging together.
Was everything lost? No, the pen strokes' impression
survived and would be readable, dried.
But the wet of my body,
the salty foam of my answer
to the midday heat,
had become part of these notes.
          My new notebook—I get one—
must be wrapped in sweat-proof plastic.

July 9.   To Matsuura

At the rest stop this afternoon
I sit with a marcher,
Tsutomu Yanagihara, under a tree
that with a cautious glance he calls *haze*.
"You get rash if you touch it."
        We sit well away from it,
        but we accept its shade.
Yanagihara mentions
women singing for peace. He likes it.
It makes him think of this year's unity
in the march.
        The march this year is backed primarily
by Gensuikyo, Communist-led,
and by Gensuikin, Socialist-led.
For fourteen years these two
antiatomic-bomb groups
have been divided, but this year
they have reunited.
Yanagihara says this rejoining
"is good." He was on a march
in nineteen fifty-nine
that was also united. Unity
"makes freedom."
        He tells me Matsuura,
our goal today,
means "Seashore abounding with pines."
In this mountainous terrain
are many slopes of pine.
A faint smell of pitch
comes occasionally in the wind,
pitch, so faint but familiar.
        Our rest time is signaled over
and we get up, we leave the *haze,*
and continue in the heat.

72

Even under clouds we feel the sun.
Hot and increasingly tired,
I think only of Matsuura. Will we ever
reach it? Can it be that it is not
an illusion, is really there
so many miles—kilometers—ahead,
this "Seashore abounding with pines"?

July 10.   The New Prefecture

1

Mrs. Fujie Fukuda
is at the morning departure meeting
in Matsuura. "I was up at five
and drove here" from Nagasaki
"in my daughter's boyfriend's car."
She has come to march with us.
She is a short woman, competent,
a Communist,
an official in Gensuikyo. I talk with her
through our today's interpreter,
Tomoko Ogata, an English teacher
in Imabuku Junior High. Mrs. Fukuda
has had long experience in the movement
and has an interest in marches,
tells me about Mao
and the Long March.
        As we fall in line to start,
a police car moves in behind us.
I ask, "Why the police?"
and Jim too is concerned.
        "They are coming to direct traffic."
        Mrs. Ogata tells the police
how we have asked about them
and they laugh. "They do not repress us,"
she says. Aoyama
waves the traffic around us at first,
but as we get into the country,
a policeman goes ahead
and helps the cars drive by.
Protected by him, our marchers
spread out and fill half the road.
        A young woman's tan and white dog
            strains on the leash, sometimes going backward,

74

so she has to carry him like a child.
The sky shows hints
of cloud radiance, hints of water,
of possible cooling. A downhill feeling.
Everywhere green, a slash of pale bamboo,
and *chandan* trees that have burnished leaves
like live oak. When not blinded by sweat,
my eyes are clear. I think of Yanagihara
who yesterday
spoke of women "singing for peace."
I ask Mrs. Ogata if her students
are organized for peace. "No," she says,
"through high school they are not allowed.
In the university they can organize."
         "In high school do they ever put on plays?"
The word "play" is hard for her,
but "drama" guides her to "play."
         "Yes, they put on plays," she says.
         "Plays connected with peace?"
         "Yes, there's one they do
called *Black Rain.* It's from the novel
by Ibuse, about this sooty rain
from the bomb." I nod. I ask,
"What's the story of the play?"
She does not know. I ask her if she'd mind
asking Mrs. Fukuda. Mrs. Fukuda:
"The main character
is a victim. He cannot do hard work
as a victim, so he fishes.
People call him lazy."
         "Do they ever sympathize with him
in the play?"
         "No, but the audience does."

2
We come to a rest stop,
some benches under trees, a picnic place.

The police rest in their parked car.
Mrs. Fukuda goes to talk with them,
her collection box hanging from her neck.
She comes back and says,
"They gave some money."

3
The march descends to the sea.
Soon we are walking along a sea wall
that has small shrimp drying on it.
The smell of shrimp and brine, then
wharfs and shoreside warehouses,
"The Sea Genkai." Jim, mad for swimming,
enthusiast of even the shallowest water,
shucks his clothes to his underpants
and plunges in while the others rest.
        Rested (this is another stop),
we hear, "Almost the end
of Nagasaki Prefecture."

4
At noon or close to noon
we reach the boundary.
An important moment.
We have now crossed
the first of the five prefectures
and are about to enter Saga.
All with us will go home.
A large group of new marchers wait,
sixty, seventy? Great cheers,
waving, the approach and threading
of our terminal group into their
beginning one, cheek touching cheek,
hair intermingling in greeting—
no kisses, but clearly
the moment's kindling warmth.

76

Speeches:

      Mrs. Fukuda makes a speech
as hearty as her stride on the road,
and our captain for the new prefecture,
Nakayama Shigetoshi, speaks,
his hair curved back
like unruly clouds. We are introduced to him,
but it is not now our new captain we want
but our old one.

      Thin Aoyama
in your yellow sweatshirt, friend
who has kept us unslippered on *tatami* matting,
who has been our substitute interpreter
in difficult moments, solving all
surprises of road and inn, table and bed,
your research ship waits.

      Sayonara, yellow leaf,
      have a good trip home.

July 10.   *Monta Tanaka*

Our interpreter for the afternoon
is Monta Tanaka, from Saga City
            still some distance ahead.
He is completely blind
and speaks excellent English.
"How did you learn it?" I ask.
            "There is not much braille in Japanese.
I made myself learn English
to have more to read. I listen
to short-wave radio in English,
to records. I use every chance
I have to speak English,
as with you." Walking companionably
between Jim and me, cane under arm,
he continues, "I make my living
as an interpreter and by teaching
in a school for the blind.
I do other things too.
Today is the national election,
so I go this evening
to read off the votes in braille."
His voice is assured. He covers
his darkness with a virile poise.

July 11.   To Arita and the Potter

1

Yesterday was the year's hottest day
in Japan and humid. Luckily
the walk by the sea eased it.
Today
three Buddhist nuns have joined us,
Ikeda Kawana, Takiko Sasaki,
and Tomiko Okumura,
all from Ushizu in Saga Prefecture.
Heads shaved, in robes of the Sangha,
they look like men until a certain sweetness
appears as they smile. "We are afraid
of becoming ill. We are not
in good health," but all day
they unceasingly beat fan drums
in time with their steps, and keep up,
though their chant is subdued.
        At the first rest, in the morning,
they talk—through our today's interpreter,
Nobuyoshi Kuga—
to Jim. It turns out they know
Hiroshi Sera, a monk
who was with Jim on the "southern walk" last year.
Their delight is evident.
They raise folded hands and bow
to give expression to their pleasure.
(They will be with us through the prefecture.)

2

On the march again,
we pass five young girls
perhaps nine years old, eye-flashers
in navy-blue uniform dresses.

Several wave. I wave and throw a kiss
and one of them throws back a kiss.
Kuga, disapprovingly,
"Children beginning to westernize."

3
Arita, the end of the day's march,
is a pottery town, its main street
lined with display windows:
plates, classic Miyazawa-blue vases
on tile bases, cups
with slender pale-green sprays
painted on their sides, the saucers
reflecting the cups.
Jim and I will lodge overnight
with a potter, Motoji Matsuo—
"You will like him."
Kuga will stay till ten o'clock obligingly
to interpret for us.
          We meet Matsuo, a tall man
springy on his feet, with hands
gesturing with modesty and clay.
We enter his cavern-like shop, passing
a box of horses. He says they are unfinished.
He still has to make saddles for them.
He is making them to sell at the Chinese
New Year because
next year is "the year of the horse."
          A cycle of twelve years, each year different.
          Year one is mouse,
          and the horse is the sixth year.
We go past rows of jars
with vine-stem handles, bowls
with celadon clouds. His potter's wheel
has fine white dust around it. Above it,
shelves of shadow and glaze.
          He brings us into his house

up a small passageway, the barrier
to dust and sound. We remove our shoes,
the barrier to the house. We meet
a tidy small bundle of woman, Mrs. Matsuo,
who mentions at once heated water—
the after-work,
the after-march rite of bathing—also
we must give her our clothes
to wash and dry overnight.
              She takes even my sweated trousers, saying
              these too will dry by morning.
Meantime I am to wear a provided
kimono, disappear into Japan.
              At dinner six of us sit
at the usual low table,
Jim and I and Kuga,
and Matsuo and his wife and a daughter,
his daughter a grown girl
wearing a thin gray sweater
with the words on it, in English,
"Try to be Active."
              As we eat,
I ask him about the horses:
Does he use a mold? Yes.
He brings the mold and takes it apart,
showing each section, legs, body, head.
At the top of the mold
is an opening. "I mix
ground stone and water and pour it in
and shake it up and down.
After twenty minutes, it's hard."
              He brings out a finished horse—
yellow body, green saddle.
"Hollow," he says. It is hollow
and light. And beautiful.
He says he dips the body in glaze—
he makes a dipping motion with his hands—
"and I paint the saddle." Then the horse

is fired. He says the Chinese potters
who worked here in Arita
did not tell all their secrets, especially
how they made colors. The Japanese
had to invent colors.
        "The word
for 'pride' in Japanese
has the same pronunciation as for 'dust,'
and I have a trade of dust." With pride
he shows us an incense burner
made in the shape of a temple
with a roof with four vents from which
"the smoke" comes out. He has us notice
the handle he designed to lift the roof—
a tiny dragon.
On the wall hangs a pottery
family emblem, a flower.
"The Emperor's emblem is a chrysanthemum."
        Emperor.
He says that his country
still has the narrowness, the pattern of feudalism.
In industry, in life
there is order, loyalty.
"Japan is well-behaved, maybe
too much so, maybe it costs us much, but
we have the advantage of order." Jim,
to illustrate his own country's difference,
tells of his forty-five arrests.
Matsuo is astonished.
He wants Jim to explain how this could happen.

4
Before we go to bed,
we sing *"Genbakuo Furusumaji"* and Matsuo
carefully
puts on his phonograph
a record of Schubert songs and hums
these immortal tunes with love.

July 12.   Next Morning

My pants are dry. I wait in kimono
as Mrs. Matsuo lays out on the floor
a legless ironing board.
Everything in Japan is on the floor. Is it
anachronism? The bare floor
of primitive man? An immortal adjunct
of the lotus position?
      Matsuo
watches his wife on hands and knees and watches
a rain of ideograms on the TV screen.
He shrugs. The conservatives
have won the election again.
      My pants ironed, I shyly put them on
under the kimono, the kimono a hint
of the "ordered" feudal past
Matsuo was telling me about. He
will march with us today. He will give up
a day's work to march for peace.
In the acacia blur of early morning
we go outside.
Neighbors are up. It's like
a small commune. They know Matsuo, know
what he is doing. I can feel it.
I hear the word *"heiwa,"* "peace."
We are "Amerikano" walking
for peace. As Matsuo refers to us,
a mother and child bow deeply,
the child's hair
falling forward over her face.

July 12. *Inadequacy During the Day's March*

No interpreter today.
At a rest stop, Matsuo
speaks with several marchers, then, for us,
puts two fingers of his right hand, spread a little,
over two spread fingers of his left hand.
We don't understand.
He makes two fists and, joining wrists,
spreads his fists. Again we don't understand,
don't know what he means. Finally
one marcher offers an English word,
"Jail." Matsuo evidently wants us
to know he has told the group
about Jim's going to jail.
The crossed fingers meant bars.
The joined wrists meant handcuffs.
But we did not have imagination
equal to his.

July 12.   Leavetaking

When we take leave, tonight,
of the marchers going home,
on an impulse of irresistible
affection *(aijo)*,
I put my arm around Matsuo's shoulder.
He pulls my hand to his mouth
and kisses it.

July 12.   *At the Hiranos*

1

Again we are taken to a private
home, this time
to that of Kunio Hirano,
a new, clean, large-roomed house
crowning a precipitate hill.
We sit with him in his "study"
while his wife, Teruko,
brings us peeled apples and tea.
I can say *arigato* now,
even *domo arigato* ("many thanks").
Hirano's sister Sumi
drops in like a flower
with a smaller flower, her daughter
Hisano. They live in the next house
down the hill, a steep path down to it,
and below, in the valley, rice fields
edged with pale red cannas like small
explosions. By Hirano's eastern windows
a sunflower.

2

We have heard that an American woman
from Colorado, Judith Hurley,
is to join us here. The phone rings.
She's coming. She comes
at twilight, a winning being,
human, speaking Japanese.
She wears a full skirt.
But she has something wrong with her feet,
which means she cannot walk with us.
She has been following, "tracking" us

from Nagasaki
to "comfort" us and give us advice.
          She tells Jim
she has heard much about him—
he drinks whiskey, he smokes cigars,
he does not eat enough, he has been
so many times jailed. "You are already almost
a legend here," she says. He smiles,
a trifle embarrassed. She says
(this is related to her advice)
that there has been some main-march dissension
over atomic power. "Gensuikyo people
are not opposed to
'the peaceful use of atomic power,'
of course, they say, provided
it can be made safe, but it's all
part of the same danger."
Her advice:
"Speak against building atomic power plants
when you can."

3
After dinner
Hirano's sister Sumi asks us
if we would like to come to her house
and "participate
in a tea ceremony." We accept.
          For Jim and me, a first.
          The tea ceremony is the essence
of traditional Japan.
Fosco Maraini, writing about it, said
that it derives from Zen Buddhist practice
and was developed, centuries ago,
both to make the Zen monk alert
and to free his mind of "contingent things,"
or irrelevancies—a kind of withdrawal—
to make him more open to thought,

to meditation, to art.
It had a social derivation too.
Socially its function
was similarly to provide a frame
of withdrawal and self-surrendering
or to give the guest the sense
of the tea-maker's marked regard.
Cha-do, the way of tea.
            Judy tells us
she has studied the tea ceremony
for fifteen years.

4

The usual place for the ceremony
is an outside pavilion or cottage
that is deliberately
kept bare and plain. The intent is
each time, with the pavilion's "things"—
furnishings, flowers, cups, bowls—
to make it new.
            Sumi has no outside cottage,
but her living room is correctly
a new arrangement.
            To one side—the one permanent thing—
a metal hearth in the *tatami* floor.
On this hearth she heaps burning charcoal
and over it sets a pot
of already boiling water.
Now the laying out
of ceremonial utensils:
a darkly glazed, large bowl
and smaller bowl-like cups,
a long-handled wooden dipper,
a jar of tea, a small white towel,
and, placed on its side,
something like my father's shaving brush
except that its bristles

are fine splints of bamboo.
The ceremony begins slowly,
every movement made with grace. Sumi
dips some hot water first and pours it,
a flash of light,
into one of the bowl-cups. She returns the dipper
to the water-pot rim and swirls
the water around in the cup and empties it
into the larger bowl. With the white towel
like a gauze, like mist,
she wipes the inside and edges
of the cup. In her slow movements
I sense an appealing hesitation as if,
though she knows the ritual,
she is not a *cha-jin,* a tea master,
but a novice just released
to the possible slight variations
of a new skill. With that skill
she reaches for the tea canister. Now
the actual making of the tea.
There are three procedures:
she takes two ladlefuls of fine-crushed tea
        ("the first and best of the crop,"
        Judy whispers to us)
and puts them in the large teacup.
Again using the dipper, she takes
a single full measure of boiling water
and pours it over the tea.
Last, she takes the bamboo-splint whisk
and, holding it vertically in the cup,
whips the tea vigorously and circularly
until it is a foaming green.
Meantime Jim has been asked to remove
a small cake from a special sealed wrapper
and eat it. This cake, Judy says,
is a preparatory taste that will heighten
the taste of the tea. Sumi
advances the tea across the matting,

bowing, and Judy
tells him to lift the bowl
in the palm of his left hand
and turn it a quarter turn with his right hand
to avoid his lip touching
the offered spot of honor. Then,
drink in three swallows. He drinks properly.
        I am next. I watch the same slow
ten-minute ceremonial preparation
of the bowl-cup of tea that at last
is slid to me across the matting.
The taste is pleasanter, blander
than I expected. In the dim light,
the charcoal softly burning and flaking, its glow
quivering on the walls, I experience
a Zen self-surrendering myself, an interior
quiet, centuries
speaking to me with unworded relevance.
Jim, appreciative,
is also responding to that quiet.

July 13.   Breakfast

Judy has slept
at Sumi's house. This morning,
having had breakfast,
she comes to talk with us at our breakfast,
which we have alone, served by Hirano's mother,
in the room where we slept.
        Judy has found out—perhaps from Sumi?—
about Hirano. He is a Communist,
local head of Gensuikyo.
He is thirty-four
and has been many years in the peace movement.
His interest started when he made visits
to "the Atomic Bomb Material Center"—
the Peace Museum—in Nagasaki.
He went to peace meetings. He attended
his first annual antibomb conference
when he was nineteen. Also,
he has an uncle, a *hibaksha,*
who died last year
of a bomb-related illness.
        He comes in as we talk.
I ask him about the Communist Party.
He says
it has eight percent of the national vote,
nineteen members in the Senate,
fourteen in the Lower House.
But he is not much interested
in national politics. "I'm interested
in local and prefectural politics.
There are great regional differences.
The Mayor of Habikino-shi
in Osaka Prefecture is Communist.
Two hundred cities have coalitions
of Communists and Socialists.

Coalitions rule in eight prefectures."
When we ask him
what he does himself, he says,
"I work on current problems."
This room we are in
has an elaborate alcove-altar.
I think, A leading Communist,
and his family is of Buddhist faith
and his sister
performs the tea ceremony.
I think,
It is evidently not
a contradiction.

July 13.   *Reminders*

Along the road today
in the open rafters of a leanto,
a swallows' nest. From it a swallow
dips out into the air
with that wing flutter so common
over the Eitzens' pond in Pennsylvania.
Further on, by a clump of bamboo,
a rose-of-Sharon is growing
like the one that shades the southeast corner
of the Gehmans' farmhouse, same ruffled
twists of white faintly stained
with spreading crimson. In this country
of continual difference, reminders
of Crow Hill.

July 13.   *Hill Scene*

Bamboo, an entire hill now
bowing in different directions
like an unorganized demonstration.

July 13.   Road Warning

On tall square gravestones
heedless lichen inching
across a few lives.

July 13.   As We Are Marching

1
As we are marching today, Jim and I
get talking with Takeshi Nakamura,
an instructor in English
in Kashima City. He teaches his students
to sing "We Shall Overcome."
And he uses a record
of Martin Luther King, Jr.
giving the speech, "I Have a Dream."
Jim says,
"I was a friend of King. I walked with him
on a march in nineteen sixty-six
in Mississippi. I wasn't a close friend,
but I knew him many years
and respected him so much."

2
Excitedly at a rest stop
the marchers want autographs
and offer Jim and me
pieces of paper, notebooks. One girl
has nothing but the inside white band
of a visor. We sign that.

3
A walker talks to me
about energy. He says,
"We use solar energy—
I mean at home—
put water on the roof to heat
and run it through a pipe to the bath.
It's usually

thirty-five degrees centigrade
and we must heat it a little more,
but once it was forty-five degrees
and we had to cool it."
He shows me a solar heater, later,
on a house we are walking past, a roof panel
whose beige waves, corrugations, are slanted
to the sun. Taking
Judy Hurley's hint, I say,
"A lot better than atomic power."
He says, "Yes," looking at it.

July 13. *What to Do in the Heat*

Often in the heat
I see Japanese men
lift their shirts to the neck
to let the torso air.
    It works.

July 14.   The Nuns

1

Of the three nuns, one is always flitting.
Errands, some responsibility
back "home"? When she goes,
the other two look nervous,
though steadily beating their drums. Today
the flitting nun is gone for some time
and comes back, having hitched a ride
behind a man on a motorcycle. She thanks him,
dismounts, adjusts her robe, and takes her place calmly
in line again, and her sister nuns
look relieved.
         A day of intermittent rain, a day
Jim likes. Rain or sweat,
we are just about as wet,
but rain cools us. If there's heavy rain,
we run for an overhanging roof
or a shed. We protect the banners.
We protect the bamboo pole
that holds thousands
of paper cranes like floating plumage.
         When the sky clears at last,
we are walking
toward a range of mountains rising
beyond kilometers of rice fields,
green above green. On the mountains
rain is still falling, curtains
almost as heavy as clouds.
The motorcycle nun drops back
and says to Captain Shigetoshi,
"Three mountains, three nuns,"
and touches her conical hat.

2

We stop for lunch near a Buddhist

temple. In a wayside restaurant I have
"yasai itame," "frizzled vegetables,"
flashing my now-adept chopsticks over them.
A nice smell of something like rose water.
Jim orders his favorite
tuna *sashimi* decorated
with green scalloped sprays.
        When we return to the temple,
we find its wide front doors opened
on a chamber of gold:
gilded altars, gilded cornice panels
with designs of leaves
and long-tailed impersonal birds.
On the *tatami*-mat floor
marchers are lying resting. Shigetoshi,
noticing us, waves us in, and I
gladly lie down with the others.
        Near us
are the three nuns, robes discarded
and their white blouses partly open.
They can be at ease here
under the dispassionate gaze
of a candle-lighted Buddha,
relax the discipline that keeps them walking
inflexibly
to their steadily beating drums.
The flitting nun has her left arm out,
rounding a cotton-sheathed breast.
The other two have their hands
pressed to their cheeks. All
sleep at home in this golden household.

July 14.   The Drum

A monk
beats his fan drum so enthusiastically
he hits Jim with the drumstick.

July 14.　　The Marchers

This afternoon
lined against a wall waiting to start,
five old women with moles, wens,
tight knots of hair, and ordinary dresses
falling straight down to ordinary
legs. Near them several working women and men
with calf-length cotton trousers
and white cloths, under their hats,
covering the backs of their necks, the sexes
like a reflection of each other.
Since marchers go only one day,
many can take off from work.
Teachers walk with us,
waving to students on the roadside
and the students wave back.
Children run along with us.
　　　　In America the walkers were special—
movement people, the dedicated.
Here they are just people.
Captain Shigetoshi tells me,
"Wave—it's good to wave."
Many pause on village streets
as we go by, interrupt talk or shopping,
and wave. A dance of arms back and forth.
An old woman with a baby waves.
A universal
sympathy, a unity.
A hand that presses
a stray hair behind the ear
holds a banner, a man who walks the street
in a blue kimono bows.
The people walk, the people watch.

July 14.   The Side Roads

Constantly
the march leaves the main highways
and turns into byways, the intimacy
of near houses, village streets:
on one street a wall hole
with a night-like glimpse
of men at furnace fires, at anvils
showering the darkness with sparks.
Now we see
a house being reroofed. A metal chute
polished from use slides old tiles
down to the unisex-clothed women working
in clouds of dust. Now a thatched roof shows
with a heavy coat of green moss.
A few thatched houses, too old to repair,
are falling into ruin. The thatch,
weakening, gaps open or drops down, letting
the thin rafters follow, collapsing
like broken ribs against the walls. Often
we pass a small crossroads shrine,
the little figure of the Buddha
scarred by time
but lit with a tin can of flowers.
Dike cannas, lilies
haunting the water, tiers of flowers,
tiers of rice. Level lawns of rice
around farmhouses. Past houses and fields,
through villages well known to the marchers,
with working drums and banners
        and collection boxes
we pursue our digressions
for peace.

July 14.   The Students

1

We enter great late-afternoon-shining
Saga City, under shade trees
past stores and offices—
        a stop at City Hall—
and so to the home
of Toyozo Kawasaki,
professor of biology. A home
on a small river in the center
of the city, a river of rocks
with muddied gray-green water
in which a large goldfish is swimming slowly,
a red ghost.

2

After dinner, three students
come from the Economics Department
of Saga University; two young men,
Toshiro Nakano and Hitoshi Omori,
and a young woman,
Sachiyo Kinjyo, nineteen,
small, beautiful with her pucker of smile.
Monta Tanaka,
our blind interpreter of four days ago,
reappears, summoned to help us.
        The meeting is for the students
to ask us questions.
Since Jim
is an activist of many years,
they direct questions to him.
He says:
"I belong to the War Resisters League.
But you should know that this is only part

of the War Resisters International,
which has branches in twenty countries,
including Japan. We believe
that 'wars will cease when men refuse to fight.'"
          He quotes this saying often, as the basic
          premise.
"Because we refuse to fight
many of us have been in jail.
I myself was in jail three years
for not fighting in World War Two."
          "You are a hero," Nakano says, from his tone
clearly meaning it.
          Jim thanks him somewhat awkwardly
and asks a question of his own.
What about students in the movement?
          Nakano says,
"There is a Student Peace Committee,
which is nationwide, but in this prefecture
there are not many members.
The All-Japan Students Union,
which has a million members,
is active for peace and against the A-bomb.
The students in the Economics Department
in Nagasaki University
are for peace."
          Sachiyo Kinjyo
says she comes from Okinawa.
"People in Okinawa
have gone through the war,
so they are active.
They are against American bases
and the Japanese Self-Defense Forces."
          Professor Kawasaki says
that of the many thousands
who will attend the August sixth
Hiroshima memorial ceremony,
"Seventy percent will be young.
The young have taken over

the struggle against the bomb."
Omori says, "Yes. Students make
excursions to Nagasaki and Hiroshima,
and in preparation the teachers
explain how these two cities have suffered.
The teachers tell us
how terrifying it was to experience
the A-bomb—"
    Nakano interrupts.
"The goverment, though,
discourages that, wants people to forget."
(Several times I have heard this.)
    Sachiyo Kinjyo
says in her low but clear voice,
"But they must be told, especially children.
The children of the next generation
will forget unless we tell them."
    Outside,
garden pines reflect a moonlight
revolving along the house
and along the street-bordering river.
As we earlier
entered the city, we went by
a lake, and turned left
under a hanging net of willows.
Saga, city of water now
shining in darkness. Across from us,
also shining,
Sachiyo Kinjyo, beautiful
small person.

July 14.   Peace Means

This friendliness of the Japanese
toward Americans. They wear
American shirts and sweaters
like Matsuo's daughter: everywhere
Jim and I see sweatshirts
with the names of American universities,
"Arkansas State University. . . Pennsylvania . . . "
True that these shirts are considered chic
in other countries, but why here?
Why this friendliness to Americans?
        Right after the A-bombing
there was rage:
"Damn them . . . damn them to hell . . . "
Then a change.
        If I understand it,
what happened was the feeling that,
like a gun, it is your life or my life;
if war exists at all,
the maximized weapon will be used.
If war as a premise is accepted,
if there can be "just wars,"
if the thinking is,
I can win if I do this,
if the thinking is,
I can delay losing if I do this,
if the thinking is,
The logic of this situation
demands this,
this will be done.
        The Japanese people now,
remembering their own past,
are in a revulsion against war,
against the military. Most
want never to fight in wars again.

Jim said it,
"Wars will cease when men refuse to fight."
A student told me,
"People must become fond of people."
Peace means
       freedom, justice, personal unselfishness,
       utopian but sane
       world lovingkindness.
It is not partial.
It is total.
Mayor Morotani said it simply enough,
"Not only nuclear weapons
but war itself should be terminated."

July 14.   Tolstoy

After the students have left, alone
in the privacy before sleep,
Jim and I talk.
I mention Tolstoy's book,
The Kingdom of God is Within You.
Jim says, "It's in the literature
we have for sale at the office,
but the title put me off. I haven't read it."
          "You might like it better than you think.
Tolstoy is hard on the churches.
Mennonites and Quakers, he's for them
but not establishment churches.
What he keeps talking about
is Matthew v 39 where Christ says
not to resist evil by force.
That's his whole argument, nonviolence."
          "Yes, but this title—"
          "I know, this 'kingdom of God' thing.
The way you feel,
that part might bother you.
He says if you're a true Christian, or
even if you just have a conscience,
there's something in you, some God-impulse of love,
that can make you nonviolent:
'The kingdom of God is within you.' That's it.
He's not a church Christian, he's a Christ Christian,
and he goes pretty far. To stop war,
he says you can't just do some minor
correcting of the system—he says the system
isn't 'corrigible.' You have to change
'the whole structure of life.'"
          "Well, that's okay,
but every time you make some big change,
communism or whatever—always

you get a new bunch of what I call
upperdogs."
    "You mean a bureaucracy."
    "I call it the boss class."
    "Well, Tolstoy's revolution
was to be nonviolent. That would make
all the difference.
It was to take away power,
substitute human goodness.
Let me tell you a story. Tolstoy
had a brother, Nicholas, his oldest brother.
When he—Tolstoy—was five,
Nicholas said he had a secret
that, if he told it, all the world
would become happy and loving. He started
a game called Ant-Brothers. Tolstoy
and his brothers crouched down under armchairs covered
with shawls and huddled together,
were Ant-Brothers. But Nicholas
wouldn't tell them the great secret.
He said he had written it on a green stick
and hidden it by a ravine.
Tolstoy remembered this all his life
and he asked to be buried
where the stick was supposed to be hidden.
That's where he was buried—
his wife and children followed his wish.
The thing is, he thought, late in life,
that he had found the secret,
that it was obeying
this God-impulse of love."
    Now the moon is wheeling
in the trees outside our room, touching them
with the light that falls
everywhere tonight.

110

July 15.   Bad Foot

1

As I came into Saga, both my feet
were blistered and painful. Overnight
my right foot swelled. In the morning,
examined and bandaged, I was ordered
to ride in the sound truck.

2

The truck is good for writing.
Shaken by its motion, I write
thoughts, escaping memories, impressions of scene
between dream and real
rice fields. Any variation of towns.
        I write
to the sound of the loudspeaker above me,
to the sound of drums behind me,
to the sound of some rhymeless, irregular
suggesting voice. I am glad
for any usable syllables
to record the charged days and their meaning.
Coleridge said,
"Poetry" must excite
"a more continuous and equal attention
than prose aims at."
But he also said,
" . . . a poem of any length
neither can be, nor ought to be,
all poetry."

July 15.   The Haras

Today we end the march
at Mitagawa, an Air Force base.
A young man, Nobuyoshi Hara, indicates
we are to come home with him. I ask,
"Do you know English?" He says, "No,
only few words."
        He drives back to Kanzaki
along the left-hand side of the road
(Japan and England) and makes
a left-hand turn into a small lane.
His home has
in front, curtained windows,
in back, the athletic field
of the Kanzaki Junior High
on which boys are playing baseball.
        Wife Sachiko
round-faced with long hair,
brings us through their *tatami*-mat living room
to a non-*tatami* alcove
that has that happy Japanese exception,
chairs. While she gets tea,
Hara tells us, helped by gestures,
that they have two small children,
a boy three and a girl one.
After tea,
he and his wife both excuse themselves,
disappearing
into another part of the house.
        In the alcove by us
is a bookcase filled with books.
I pull one out: R. M. Rilke
and a photograph of Rilke.
Thin, high-quality pages
that pass under the finger like scorings

of music: columns
of ideograms. I think, Somewhere here
is *"Wer, wenn ich schriee, hörte mich . . . ?"*
Hara has returned. He is pleased
at my interest in his books
and shows me volume after volume:
Goethe. Tolstoi. Dostoievski.
Balzac. Flaubert.
DeMaupassant. Sartre. Gide, Camus.
Shakespeare.
Dickens, Faulkner, Steinbeck.
All in Japanese. And he motions to
a reproduction on the wall of a nude,
"Renoir," the flesh
bringing its sun-sleeping curves
from France here
to Saga Prefecture.
        He tells us he is now leaving us
to get his children: "Bring in car." They are
in a school for little children—
he shows "little" with his hand.
        "Nursery school," I say, and he nods.
He comes back a few minutes later
carrying Satomi, his daughter,
who clings to him. Her hair is long
like her mother's. Shiro, the boy,
has his hair cut short
and he and Satomi
both have serious round faces.
We can't talk with them, but Jim
hides behind a partition
and reappears, his international peek-a-boo
at last making Shiro laugh.
        After the mandatory bathing,
family dinner is in the kitchen
at a western-style table. In our honor
Sachiko has prepared
a Japanese-American dinner;

Jim's *sashimi,* but also
hamburgers drenched with onions and a bowl
of potato salad.
        I watch Shiro, the three-year-old, eat.
He holds his chopsticks clenched
in his fist, yet opens and closes them
perfectly, grasping the potatoes
firmly. He dumps catsup on his hamburgers
like an American child.
        After dinner Sachiko
undresses him and he runs around
in only a towel, kicking his legs
splendidly but still serious.
Satomi is serious too, and admiring. Sachiko
interrupts the admiration
and puts them both to bed.
        It is soon time
for us to go to bed too.
Sachiko spreads mattresses
on the living-room floor, flicking
a single sheet over each
with a least hint of folding under. Then,
"Good night,"
and we are left to the room's darkness, as
from the alcove windows white curtains
blow inward in great
grasping curls, touching
the backs of Rilke,
Camus, Shakespeare, Faulkner.

July 16.   The Golf Course

This afternoon we pass by
a golf course, the first I've seen.
I'm told it's private,
that there are no public courses.
I watch the green of the long "holes," and I'm troubled.
This kind of green in this country
goes against the need for rice.

July 16.   Rice

Japan is rice. With passion
monks and disciples
eat any rice Jim and I
leave on our plates. They even regularly
put tea on their plates to wash any remnants
into their mouths. Nothing is wasted.
         The raising of rice is as avid
as eating it. A paddy
may seem to end but will round a corner
and quick send out a further meter
of green. The rampant
green divisions march to the sea. Rice
is the white flood. Everywhere
its ankle-wetted stalks make terraces
mirrors of water unnaturally climbing
the hills.
         If the fields go up,
the water comes down, from the highest paddies
trickling down to the lowest. I ask a marcher
if the water is pumped. He says,
"Usually not. Usually
it comes from springs or streams."
         In most paddies
are partitions, dikes, raised narrow earthworks,
lines of diagrams. You see
farmers in hip boots sheering off the weeds
that grow on these dikes, using
a powered rotary blade. Many farmers
plant beans, eggplant on the dikes
and add a rim of wealth.
         Some dikes are paths.
Gyotsu Sato told me
that when he walked a dike as a boy, often
frogs jumped into the water. He said

116

some kind of small fish—loach—
is bred in the fields. The loach eat grubs
and when the water at last is drained,
they fall obligingly into nets
for a further crop. The water
is only drained shortly before harvest.
      Yoshie Tentaku told me,
"We have a saying, 'The riper rice is,
the more it bends its head.' That means,
the more successful you become,
the more modest you should be,"
and she drew two pictures for me,
one of the rice when it's young,
the other when it's ripe and bending
"like greeting somebody very courteously."
      I will not be here for that bending harvest,
but I have seen the green plants
answer to the wind in waves that are
a universality of tone, a surf
alert on the shores of hunger.

July 16. Jim's Rest

After the golf course, after many fields
and several villages, comes the rest stop,
and Jim lies down on his stomach,
head on arm, at the side of the road.
I ask him if he's all right.
      "I'll be all right. It's my ulcer."
      He tells *me*. He doesn't tell others
or want me to tell them. Just once, before,
he mentioned "ulcer," *"kaiyo,"*
and panic. The then captain
and several aides wanted at once
to rush him to the hospital.
No. He was adamant. No hospital.
Kaiyo was an old friend.
Nothing to do but be patient, wait.
It had come. At its own pleasure
it would go. He had brought some pills,
and they and a private conversation
with the ulcer would be enough.
      Now as the line reassembles,
he gets up and takes his place in it.

July 16. Night

Tonight I ask Jim
how he is. He says, "Better.
I've taken a couple of pills
and it's let up. The hot bath
was a big help. Great thing,
this Japanese soaking-tub."
        "You ought to be on some regimen."
        "But the ulcer goes away.
Don't worry, it goes away."
        As the early night quiets,
we drift into a continuation
of our Saga talk on nonviolence. Jim says,
"This country is really okay,
spends less than one percent of the GNP
on arms. One marcher
bragged to me about it. He knew.
What's not so good is this Self-Defense Force.
It reminds me a lot
of Core and Snick, how they switched
from nonviolence to 'black power,'
how they talked about 'self-defense.'
What they meant was violence.
I'd say to them,
'You giving up on King?' I'd ask,
'When have riots or violence
done any good?' I'd say,
'Tell me just one time it has,'
and they never could. But nonviolence . . .
The lunch-counter sit-ins
desegregated the eating places.
Freedom Rides desegregated travel.
The nineteen sixty-three March on Washington
won the civil-rights law.
Selma won the voting-rights law.

I could name plenty more. So could you.
But we can't explain these things here
to the Japanese, with the language,
and they don't know the background."
He punches his sleeping-bag pillow
to make it soft. He lets his head down.
"People ask me—even Paula would—
if it was worthwhile, three years in jail,
the freedom-ride beating.
I always say, 'Yes, it was.'"

July 17.   *Kanji and Toyoko*

1

Children often march with us.
Today, a Sunday, we have two,
Kanji Nishimura,
a boy of five,
and Toyoko Sinohara, somewhat older,
a girl in a white hat
who stays close to her mother. Kanji
runs up and down the line of march
as if he was the march captain. But later
he tires and rides in the car.
       I too am in the car
       with my bad foot.
The driver, Hiroyuki Hasegawa,
for ten years has been a teacher
in Saga Nogei High School,
his subject, agriculture. I say,
"Do you teach how to grow rice?"
He nods.
       In the distance
I hear a sound like children cheering.
I look for a possible playground.
Instead we come
to some long buildings, chicken coops,
in which at least a thousand hens
are announcing they have laid eggs.
Little Kanji's ear evidently
has not confused them with children.
As we leave the coops behind,
he says a few satisfied words
to Hasegawa.

2

At Kiyama we reach the end

of Saga Prefecture. My foot
is good enough now
to let me walk into town with Jim:
important that the two Americans
head the march and be seen together with
the Japanese against the bomb. Kanji
frisks along with us.
        The contingent awaiting us
from the new prefecture, Fukuoka,
is large and lively, expectant. We meet
the new prefecture captain,
Yosinori Yosihara, and again
I have that sense of lift and life.
As the equipment is exchanged,
Yosihara distributes
every last collection box
to the younger marchers, speaking to them
in a tone of humor and challenge.
        Now
time for the prefecture farewells.
I say goodby to Captain Shigetoshi
and to the nuns
who bow low and shake my hand.
They are especially tender with Jim,
Sera's friend. But across from them,
new nuns, monks, and drums are waiting.
And across from Kanji
who gives me a firm handshake
and Toyoko who gives me a shy one,
five children are waiting.
It's the new prefecture,
something keyed-up, Fukuoka promising
a special drive,
a dimension.

July 17.   Sugawara Michizane

At a meeting this evening
in Chikushino City, Captain Yosihara,
after asking Jim about his work, asks me
about my writing and I mention
poetry. One says,
"This city has a famous poet
who lived a thousand years ago,
Sugawara Michizane.
There is a shrine to him
near the great Dazaifu Shrine.
Would you like to see it?"
Jim and I say that we would.

      We are driven to a large vacant space,
a level lonely mini-plain, a place
spectacularly bare. Around it, hills.
On the ground, strung with struggling grass,
three rows of stones, bases of columns.
Behind them, sanded rectangles
where other buildings once stood.
An enclosed poster shows the design
of these buildings. Not restoring them,
not rebuilding them,
is a tribute, honoring
the poet by keeping only this last fragment
of his home.

      As I look, from this hinted home,
up into the hills:
      "Above there
is a castle in ruins that once defended
this city against the Mongolians."
      Michizane's singing here, and up there
      Tu Fu's other
      "unhappy music."

July 18.   *Hustler Yoshihara*

1

Today in a Kasuga civic structure
we have lunch
brought for all of us, sitting in concentric
circles on the floor: trays of cucumbers,
tomatoes, rice balls. And something like knishes
that Captain Yoshihara calls
"potato croquettes." He sits beside me.
The collection boxes are piled in a corner.
On each relay of the march
a dozen or more young men and women
run with the boxes. One girl
runs with a particularly appealing
body swing, box in her left hand,
her right hand free—runs or paces
tirelessly, up side streets, into back yards,
into stores. She holds out her collection box, smiling
in a rush of pleading, and hurries on.
All the boxes rush. They must keep up
with the marching line and still
make these pleading stops, run
up outside staircases. Yesterday
in one afternoon they collected
a hundred thousand yen,
"four hundred dollars."
            Yoshihara has some English.
I say, "How the young people run!
Why are you Fukuokans so good? Better than Saga?
More people, collect more money—
run, run?"
            "Saga." His expression says,
Saga's not Fukuoka.
He stands up and in his commanding
and humorous voice repeats to the room

124

what I said.
Laughter. In the back of the room now
the morning's money is being counted,
stacked in neat piles of coins and bills. Soon
the collective collected total is announced.
"A hundred twenty-five thousand yen."
It's clear
Fukuoka Prefecture hustles.

2
Outside, on a grassy bank,
a young man sits soaking his tired feet
in a pond. Tired
but he is going
to run again.

July 18.   The Enokidas

Some marchers now march more than one day.
Tomekichi Enokida
has been in the march two days
with his wife. He and she
hold the identifying streamer between them,
HEIWA KOSHIN (PEACE MARCH). And walk in front.
Easy to see they are in love.
    At the day's end
at Fukuoka City's city hall
(two hundred fifty people and speeches)
I talk with him.
His father and mother were both victims
in Nagasaki. His father died,
his mother is in a hospital,
but he says it is not just because of them
that he joined the peace movement.
It was his own feeling.

July 18.   *Jim and the Bases*

In Kasuga before lunch
we had passed an Air Force base,
a long wall, a soldier on guard
at a gate. At lunch
Jim said, "Let's go back,
let's have a demonstration." Yosihara
reported this to the marchers
sitting on the floor. They sympathized
with Jim, but showed no sign
of any intention to go back.
After lunch our long column
passed another Army base,
an endless fence, at the gate
five soldiers, on a parking lot
a phalanx of jeeps. Again
no demonstration.
        In the evening
in Fukuoka City
about thirty men and women
have dinner with us. They tell about themselves.
Most are union people.
One is S. Kuroiwa,
"Secretary-General
of the A-Bomb Sufferers Association
of Fukuoka City."
Two are Communists, so
identifying themselves. Jim asks,
"Are you sympathetic
to China or the Soviet Union?"
        "We're independent," they say.
        A woman asks if it is true,
what she has heard,
that Jim was jailed forty-five times.
Jim says yes and explains about

civil disobedience
in the United States and "police harassment."
He tells how on the "southern walk"
while he was with it
they were "busted"—arrested—four times.
He says the walkers
were mostly black, so the arrests
were "racial." In one jail
the whites and blacks were segregated
"and the two Japanese walking with us
were put in cells with the blacks."
Some sober looks now among the listeners.
       But the talk lightens. Yosihara
returns to Jim's suggestion
about having a demonstration
at the Army base at Kasuga
and possibly getting arrested.
"We're sorry," he says, smiling,
"to have deprived you of your hobby."

July 18.   In the Coffee House

1

After dinner Jim and I
go for a quiet coffee
with Yosihara and three union men:
Junzo Umezu, President
of the Fukuoka City employees labor union,
and Hiroshi Okada
and Takamitsu Ohtsuka,
two officials in the union.
Okada says, pointing to Umezu
and joking, "He's my boss."
Ohtsuka says, after him,
"My boss too." Yosihara:
"My boss is the Japanese people."

2

Ohtsuka was born in Isahaya
in 1937. The day
the atomic bomb was dropped,
he was walking in the mountains
about twelve miles from Nagasaki.
Seeing the *pika* and hearing
the delayed sound of an explosion,
he ran to a cave. He stayed there
an hour. "When I came out,
I saw pieces of paper
falling from the sky. The bomb
took the papers up in its draft
and scattered them. And some ash was falling.
I was only eight and I was frightened."
Frightened
even twelve miles away. Later he saw
the leveled city.

July 19.   At Kyushu University

When we start today's march many strong
from the same Fukuoka City City Hall
where we ended up last night,
we are accompanied by the enchanting
slight modulation of the Buddhist chant
and drum.
                    A fan drum
                    is different tapped at the edge or lightly hit
                    in its outer circle. Its full sound
                    issues as if from a rounded mouth
                    from the center.
We wind our way
past high-rise buildings, past indefinite
morning yards
to Kyushu University. Here
a sign with a dove flying across it
and under the dove, a line of characters:
"Against Nuclear Weapons." Another line:
"Welcome, Peace March."
And on the sign a long red band, like a road,
maps our route from Nagasaki
to Hiroshima. The sign,
prepared by the Teachers Union, touches us.
As we go through the university grounds
under trees,
past entrances with students waving and calling,
past open windows crowded with
an enthusiasm of black hair,
we call and wave too. Our banners dip.

July 19.   *Hiroshima* Hibaksha (*Victim*)

In the outskirts of Fukuoka City,
a hospital for A-bomb victims.
Outside it stands a man whom Yosihara
talks with and brings to me,
Haruhiko Eguchi.
Eguchi says he has been two years
in the hospital. On August 6,
in Hiroshima, he was only
nine hundred meters from the hypocenter
(a half mile) but was by a pond.
He believes having water near him
and having the shelter of garden walls
saved him. He shows me burns behind his ears
and on his wrists that are swollen still,
and on his shoulders. I catch the word "dreams."
Yosihara says, "He dreams
always in an atomic situation." Now
Eguchi covers his wrists and burned shoulders
as the marchers sympathetically
crowd around him. They tell him,
"We want to ban the bomb."
Even if the bomb is banned,
even if the horror is abolished,
what about Eguchi?

July 20.   *The Photographs*

Last night we reached Koga, marching
with Yosihara to a small
open-air shrine. On its steps, the young people
emptied their collection boxes
to count the day's take, transcendent bankers
kneeling in sunlight, girls and boys together.
    And this morning, at the shrine, are many
of the same collection-box hustlers. As they wait,
Yosihara brings from the sound truck
nine large photographs
and lays them out on the shrine steps:
the Hiroshima atomic bomb exploding;
Hiroshima after the bomb;
a man with the dark lines of his kimono
fire-stenciled into his back;
a small boy and his older brother
lying burned and still;
victims, their clothing burned or torn from them,
floating in a river.
Other indelible visions.
Those waiting with collection boxes
glance at the photographs, glance away.
Today
they will run hard.

July 20.   *Chain Massage*

On the shrine steps
a girl sits with a boy
behind her massaging her neck and shoulders.
Behind the boy another boy
sits massaging the first boy's shoulders, help
for running well.

July 20.   Double Duty

For a while the march
is along a houseless mountain highway. Here,
since the marchers cannot use their boxes
to get money, they lift them
to show their slogans to the approaching traffic.

July 20.   Okagaki

1

The march today ends at Okagaki,
but Jim and I do not stay there.
We spend the night
at Daifuku Inn at Ebitsu
on a beach on a bay on Gen-Kai.
Jim, water-enthusiast,
at once drenches his skin in salt waves quieted
behind a breakwater.

2

At dinner
we have as interpreter
Miss Nobuko Ishida. Near her sits
the local head of Gensuikyo,
Mitutosi Hosokawa, wearing
soft pants and a plain shirt.
I ask him with Miss Ishida's help
how he got into "the movement."
My asking is a formality—
I expect an answer like others,
but instead he begins to tell
a story.
          Near here the American Army
twenty-seven years ago
(not long after the war)
established a base for military
exercises. To do that
they cut down a triangle of pines.
"Beautiful pines," he says,
"and needed by farmers as a windbreak." Local life
was soon being interfered with,
and he began to organize protest. At first

the movement was small,
but the provocation grew. Fishing
was an essential local "work."
"The noise of bombs and shooting
made it hard to catch the fish.
Students could not study in school.
They complained to the government,
and at considerable expense
the government soundproofed some schoolrooms."
  When the United States entered
the Vietnam War,
war exercises accelerated.
A military jet plane fell,
destroying a farmhouse, luckily
with nobody home, but a hundred
nearby homes were damaged, windows broken,
walls gashed by scattering debris.
There were many smaller accidents.
Bullets strayed through farmhouse and school windows.
Sometimes a shot came
while students were playing on the school grounds.
People became "very nervous."
They fled "many times" from the fields.
Then occurred the incident
that had been almost sure to happen.
The shooting range had signs: KEEP OFF,
but two people, not noticing them,
wandered on and were killed.
Because there were signs,
there was no compensation. These deaths,
continuing stray shots, noise,
exploding bombs: by now
the protest movement had grown
until ninety percent of the people
in Okagaki were in it.
  At the base entrance
they erected a shelter, a roof
from which hung protective

136

transparent sides.
"Here is a photograph of it.
You can see our people in it."
This shelter stayed in place a month,
and then a permanent cottage was built
further out on the main road
to be a center for the protest.
Six years ago under this pressure
"the American Army finally
left, but then
the Japanese Self-Defense Forces
came here and began exercising
and we realized it was a deliberate substitute
for the Americans. They control them."
The protest continued just as strong
until
the government recently promised
to remove all forces "next spring,
to completely evacuate the base."

3
Hasokawa's story told
and dinner finished,
he and Miss Ishida leave. Jim and I
sit on the *tatami* matting
by our low-silled windows,
looking out at bay and sea,
at lights beyond the breakwater,
        fishing boats?
and at a passing tumult of clouds.

July 21.   A Morning Ride

1

In the morning
Miss Ishida returns with Hosokawa
and takes Jim and me
to see the Mayor of Okagaki,
Morizou Isugi.
The Mayor's office is cool. He sits behind his desk
and at once signs for us
the United Nations appeal against the bomb.
He is a large, kindly-faced man.
As he talks with us, I tell him
I am seventy-one.
Smiling, he says he too
is seventy-one. I say
my mother lived to ninety-three.
He says his mother too
lived to ninety-three.
Pleased by the coincidences, he comes forward
and says to me, "The same age,"
pointing to his nose, the Japanese way
of pointing to oneself.

2

After the visit to the Mayor,
Miss Ishida takes us
on a short drive to see
the places Hosokawa last night
told us about. First,
across a wide rice paddy,
the low facades of two hospital buildings
and a row of old farmhouses
with dripping eyeless eaves.
Hosokawa says,

"That's where the jet plane crashed."
        Now we go up some steep roads
to a temple. The temple
has a large level parking lot. We park
and climb steps past water tinkling
over a stone—this is shrine water with dippers—
to the temple, the usual
cavern of gold. From a ledge beside it,
like an echo of the parking lot,
we look out on the cycloramic valley;
the bare-earth triangle
of the army base cleared in the woods,
the fine-edged texture of pines, and beyond that
Ashiya Air Base on the horizon.
Hosokawa says that that air base
is the one the crashed plane came from, and is
"a base for atomic weapons."
Jim says, "We hear no noise
anywhere, no shooting."
        "The exercises have been stopped
until the Peace March goes by."
        We drive again down into the valley.
We pass the cottage for protest.
It stands at the edge of a rice paddy,
and across its front are Japanese characters
in strong vertical lines.
"What do they say?" Jim asks Miss Ishida.
        "'Self-Defense Forces, leave.
Return the base to our inhabitants.'"

July 21.   A Family for Peace

Miss Ishida says,
"My whole family works for peace.
My parents and my brother Yasutaka.
They belong to the local peace committee.
My brother works for the small-scale
industrial workers union
and works too for the poor,
for people with heavy taxes.
He and his wife
help them calculate their tax,
so they will know what to pay."
        At a meeting at Onga
I meet Miss Ishida's mother and father.
Her father is on the city council
and gives a speech of greeting. Afterward
I come up to him to shake his hand.
I put out my hand. He does not move.
His wife says, *"Amerikano,"*
and tells him I want to shake his hand. Quickly
he puts out his hand and I take it.
        He is blind.

140

July 21. What we Heard in Kitakyushu

We arrive in Kitakyushu,
a city of a million population,
in late afternoon. Super-industry,
iron and steel, cement, petrochemicals.
Every kind of factory chimney, even
three metal tubes rising together,
joined at the top, looking
like a simplified Eiffel Tower.
This chimney has been designed, I hear,
to clean smoke, is "antipollution."
 We reach an open square
filled with children, four- or five-year-olds—
a few older—preparing to pull
a festival float. Here we stop
and here our new captain, Shintaro Kagawa,
tells me a story:
 When the Americans atom-bombed Nagasaki,
their target of choice had been
here, right here in Kitakyushu,
this much larger city
where *Bock's Car* had been ordered to hit
the arsenal in the Kokura district,
but an accidental fire and smoke
and cloud overcast
hid it. They circled three times
and, not finding the ordered target
and fuel running low, they left
for the secondary target,
Nagasaki. So children
like these waiting at the float rope
were not killed.

July 22.   The Taxi

We will be in Kitakyushu City
for two more days, to go through
all its five districts:
Yahata which includes Kurosaki where we first
arrived by the festival float,
Tobata, Kokura, Wakamatu, and Moji.
         A monk
joins us today with five companions,
one a small boy, Nobuhiro Abe,
accompanied by his father,
so again with drums
we walk through this early morning
saved city.
         A taxi passes. On its roof
the trademark of the taxi company,
a dove with spread wings.

July 23.   Moji Station

At noon and still in Kitakyushu,
half a hundred new marchers
meet us at Moji Station.
Among them is a man
with white hair, thin and fine,
down the back of his neck. Yet
he looks young. He takes my hand.
His name is Yojiro Taya.
I tell him I am seventy-one.
He says he is seventy-six
and again takes my hand.
"Haiku," he says. He explains
through our interpreter,
"For fifty-five years
I have been walking around Japan
writing haiku."
           "What kind?" I ask him.
           "All kinds. Country scenes,
nature, the seasons, but mainly
in the last twenty years
haiku against war."
           "And now you're marching with us."
           "Every year I've marched
in demonstrations against war.
I march and write.
I've written thousands of haiku." Seventeen syllables,
each a breath
against death.

July 24.   The Ferry

1

Today in the afternoon
we take the ferry from Moji
to Shimonoseki. Jim says,
"Farewell to Kyushu." I think,
It is goodby and we may never
see Kyushu Island again.
        In the strait we pass ships, the *Solar Peak*
and the *Evergrand,* an American ship
flying the Panama flag, tied
to a barrel-like buoy.
Ahead, the Kanmon Bridge,
its spare white suspension
high above the water, and beyond it,
the Tsushima Strait.
            Far up on the Kyushu side a monk
            points out to me a dome
            with a mast-like extension above it,
            the largest Buddhist peace pagoda
            in Japan, a Fujii hemisphere.
Our quick ferry
rocks as we go through waves,
and the chairs on the upper deck
rock too, thump, thump.
Leaning over the side,
we watch the pleasant froth of our wake.
We breathe sea air.

2

Soon
we are gliding with a slow wash
to the ferry dock. Mooring lines
are thrown on the cleats. Passengers,

144

marchers step carefully
over the gap between deck and dock.
      Honshu,
Yamaguchi Prefecture,
and Honshu's reception group greet us
with particular warmth as we line up
before them for the ritual
passing of equipment. Now
more than before,
more than in any evening transfer,
more than in any prefecture transfer,
here on the cobbled shore of Honshu,
an embrace of banners.

July 24.　　*Nobuhiro Abe*

For a number of days, eight-year-old
Nobuhiro Abe marched with us.
His father Yoshio was with him,
but Nobuhiro walked with the Buddhists,
beating a fan drum. His round eyes
had a child's liquid look,
but he asked no consideration
as a child and at no time hinted
any complaint. He wore a red cap
that had "United States of America"
in a curve in front. Under the curve,
an emaciated eagle. Under the eagle,
the single word, "Apollo."
He had bare legs and gaudily
decorated little sneakers.
　　　　Just before we took the ferry
to Shimonoseki, our group
held a discussion at a long table
like a board meeting. It was evidently
about policy and dull.
It went on for an hour.
Many became hopelessly drowsy.
Heads dropped down, eyes closed.
Nobohiro fell fast asleep,
his head on the back of his chair,
his face pointing to the ceiling.
A woman gently fanned him.

July 24.   A Conversation with Yuko Tomita

Yuko Tomita is today's
volunteer interpreter, a junior student
at Kitakyushu University.
I ask her about herself.
She tells me her father is dead
and her mother and an aunt
run an inn in Shimonoseki,
the Tomitaya. She says, *Ya,"*
the syllable-word
added to the family name, Tomita,
"means house, store, or inn.
Shimonoseki's not a resort,
so there are not many tourists,
but businessmen come and stay
one or two nights."
          Yuko
has a younger sister, Noriko,
who works as a bank teller.
"She buys me cakes when she gets paid.
In Japan one is paid once a month.
She helps Mother with money
and helps me with money for college.
I sometimes wash and cook for her.
My friends laugh at me because
she is my younger sister
and usually the younger sister
does such things for the older, so this
is the opposite of custom.
I wash and cook for the inn too."
          "What do you cook?
          "Spaghetti, omelette,
tomato soup, *yakimeshi*. But always
I've wanted to speak English.

When I was just
a student in junior high,
I tried to be an airplane stewardess,
to go where English was spoken.
I took the test, but I failed.
Many Japanese girls dream
of being stewardesses,
but the test is hard.
Then I wanted to go to college.
Mother wouldn't let me until
I worked a year in a bank
to save money, and then asked her
again and again, then
she let me go. At the bank
I was an information clerk
at the head office and talked
with English-speaking persons when they came
to change money. In college now
I'm studying English, but the classes
teach grammar and reading,
not conversation, so I've joined
a club, the E.S.S.,
the English-Speaking Study Club.
It has four sections: drama,
discussion, debate, and giving speeches.
I'm in the debate section.
I've debated twice."
        "What were the subjects?"
        "'Euthanasia' and 'The Right to Strike.'"
        "Tell me about 'The Right to Strike.'
Isn't it legal to strike?"
"Yes, but not railway workers
or public employees. If railway workers
strike, they keep people from traveling.
But what happens is
they strike for the right to strike."
        "Then you believe in the right to strike."
        "Yes, I took the affirmative."
        "Did you win?"

148

She shakes her head no.
"I'm in my third year.
For two years I went to school at night.
This was a problem, no time to study.
I just took a test this March
to enter day classes. I passed.
Out of twenty-eight, six passed.
That made me very happy.
It may be I will teach English.
If I do I'll have time to study.
I can even save and go abroad
and learn to talk."
        She has her own
definite thoughts about war:
"We must never use the A-bomb or make war
even if it's to make peace."
She means the many
who say armaments are "for peace."
"Arms on one side make for arms
on the other, so what to do
is not to arm, but try to understand
people in other countries.
If one country has nuclear weapons,
another country has to have them
'for defense,' but even if the aim
is defense, we don't need them.
The Japanese constitution
says we mustn't have weapons ever,
but now under the status quo we have
the Japanese Self-Defense Forces.
It's the same thing. It's weapons,
it's for war."
        "Do other students feel this way?"
        "Some do but not all,
so we have to trust—hope—
enough people in other countries
will feel this way. The trouble is
not many people are needed to kill,
just one who presses a button."

July 25.   *Pillows*

What can be revealed by pillows?
Throughout our march
Jim and I have been astonished
by the Japanese pillow. Small and hard,
it pains the ear and creaks.
Jim rejects it entirely and puts
his sleeping bag under his head.
I put the pillow under my mattress,
making a soft bulge for my head.
Talking with Yuko, I decided
that, daughter of an innkeeper,
she could tell me about pillows. I asked her.
She said, "You know Japanese
sleep on their backs. A hundred years ago
people slept on wooden pillows.
Now only a few old people do.
When I was little—you say 'knee-high'?—
I tried a wooden pillow.
I had difficulty with it.
But we use a hard pillow,
keeping that much of tradition."
        "What is the pillow stuffed with, then?"
        "Buckwheat husks," she said.

July 25.   Japan Sea Solo

Today in Shimonoseki
Jim and I are divided.
We are put in separate cars.
"You will meet again later."
The driver of my car
is Fumiaki Sato.
Takeo Yamamoto
is with us. We drive rapidly
away from the main line of march,
which borders the south of Honshu,
and go up along the Japan Sea,
along islands on which trimmed pines,
gaps at intervals between their limbs,
stand like old drawings,
or rocks seethe in the water.
"This is Kitaura."
      All day, at top speed,
we go from town to town,
visiting city halls, Yamamoto
taking me in—talking his way in—
introducing me to mayors
and getting eight or nine signatures
to the antibomb appeal.
Also getting contributions.
Hohoku, Toyoura, Kikugawa.
      From the Japan Sea we take back roads
through Honshu's mountains, ridge beyond ridge
raised
like shoulders of shadow.
The woods and vegetation
come to the road on either side,
precipitously blocking the upward view
in places,
and the mountains, as they reappear,

are like an extended
Mount Monadnock and Gap,
except all are green to the top.
There is no end to this green.
At times pines or other woods
have been cut. New plantings are put in,
and the even rows of trees on some hills
are like the upward reflections of rice.
        In Toyota
we stop at a private house for lunch,
the home of a young woman,
Kazuyo Okafuji,
who prepares lunch for us
and sits and eats with us.
        After lunch
we walk with her through the narrow streets
past sliding windows and laughter
like Kabuki scenes
and come to the town hall and the mayor.
After our business there,
we walk back through the continuing laughter,
through midday heat to our car.
        We drive now to the strait and at the strait
see the hills of Kyushu again
far off across the water in a mist.
By the Kotogawa River
we find the march resting.

July 25.   *Hashi*

Marching with us
is Hiromichi Hashiguchi,
called for short, "Hashi."
A Buddhist, he has lived in India
and in Sri Lanka, studying.
He has miniature elephants
sent him from Sri Lanka.
The Bodhisattva rode an elephant,
and these miniatures, very small,
are good for traveling, so
he gives them to us to wear.
The one he gives me
has eyes like flowers
and a large flower saddle.
He tells me his father was also
a Buddhist, dead four years ago.
He was a soldier in China.
        "A Buddhist and fighting?"
        "It was compulsory conscription, then.
If you refused to fight,
you were jailed; so, many Buddhists,
though unwillingly,
entered the army. The military were ruthless."
        With Hashi are three young Buddhists,
Araki, Hozo, and Saito.
        Hashi graduated in the Arts
at Tokyo University. As a student
he was a Communist, a party member
active in organizing miners
and in demonstrations. At that time
the party was the only
antiestablishment group
students had available.
Later he saw the party's "faults"

and in India found Fujii Guruji.
Buddhism was long an institutional
religion. In old times the monks
set up a power corresponding
to merchants and warriors
and held and defended lands.
Buddhism then
became much like any
conservative Protestant sect
"in the United States," but Fujii,
militantly proselytizing
(those strong eyes), tried to reanimate
pure Buddhism.
  In India
Hashi learned the drum
and the undeviating tenet
"not to kill."
  He is married. He and his wife
Mieko and their children
live in a commune
south of Miyazaki on Kyushu.
With him there
has been a brother-in-law,
Mino de Angelis, an American,
who will soon join us.
And some of their children
will join us too.
There is an excitement now.
We are nearing Hiroshima.

July 25.　　　Ube, Six in a Room

Tonight we are six in a room
with the indefinitely expandable house count
of the Japanese inn. The six
are Hashi and his three Buddhist friends
and Jim and I. All the room sides—
there are no outside windows—
are filled with drying clothes.
　　　　　After dinner, Jim
spreads his mattress bed, drinks whiskey,
and goes at once to sleep.
　　　　　Hashi
takes a small square table—
Japanese chess, *shohgi*—
down from a shelf and he and Hozo
arrange the ivory pieces like phalanxes
ready for battle. On another shelf
a similar table with two bowls
of round pieces, black and white—
igo, checkers—
"Also a good game," Hashi says.
　　　　　Later, beds are prepared,
rows of mattresses evenly
aligned on the *tatami* mats.
The Japanese pillows are laid down.
I watch to see
if the Buddhists sleep on their backs.
Yes, all lie on their backs, their heads
on the hard pillows. What Yuko told me
is so. Through partitions
a light shines from two sides,
softened by the opaque paper.
Sliding partitions, I think. Tired,
I slide myself to sleep.

July 26.   *Yamaguchi*

Another day in a rapid car
visiting city halls not reached
by the marchers:
a road-intersection stone lantern,
the partly shaved swathes of hills, in these swathes
the new plantings padded with straw.
           We end the day's tour
in Yamaguchi Prefecture. Here
five Americans join us,
come down through Honshu
on the "feeder walk" from Tottori
to be with us from here on:
Marguerite and Richard Tirk,
their niece Betsy, Joyce Dostole,
and Chip Poston, a vegetarian
bearded like the Amish but not Amish,
who meditates.
And Hashi and friends are with us,
and now a new march captain, for the first time
a monk, Hideo Morioka
whom I met last year in New York.
He will be with us all the way
to Hiroshima. To the Sangha temple there.
Now there will be
a new substantiality of chants.

July 26.   *Father and Son*

At the inn tonight
I go down to wash my clothes
in the bathroom
at a tap of warm water there.
        It's a large bath to accommodate
many men. Near me,
as I work naked in the heat,
is a heavy-set Japanese
and his thin son. It's late. They are
the only other ones here, the father
washing his small son. First he takes him
slantwise across his lap
and washes his face, both he
and the boy making sounds
that are words but also definitely
love sounds. The man stands the boy up
and soaps him all over, head to foot,
every part of him white with soap,
then dips a pan of water
from the communal tub
and pours it over the boy.
The boy takes another pan
and pours water down his own back.
He speaks through the water murmur,
and again, the sound of love.

July 27.   *The Third Tour*

I am once more assigned to a car
to canvas town halls, the driver and leader
Toshiaki Fujiwara
and accompanying him one of the Buddhists,
Takeji Araki. Takeji
tells me with some amusement that Fujiwara
is a Yamaguchi
tax collector. We take
an incessantly beautiful
road over the mountains
and come to the Shuho town hall.
Waiting downstairs (there is always
a wait before we see the mayor),
we notice a panel on the wall.
It has four sets of figures.
The town's total population: 8574.
The number of males: 4076.
The number of females: 4498.
The number of houses: 2383.
"There are more women than men,"
I say. "Is that from war?"
        Takeji says, "Partly, but in Japan
the large cities have more men,
the small towns more women."
        When we have seen the officials,
Hiroshi Fujimoto
comes out with us and takes the driver's seat
in a jeep in which he will guide us
to two city halls,
Mine City and Mitoo. We follow him
and come to a place of dust,
a cement plant using a special stone
from a series of hills. Trucks
run along the summits of these hills

as if along parapets. Samurai
could be standing guard there in feudal turrets.
Below, dust eddies from the crushers.
            In Mine City town hall,
as the mayor is coming out, he is putting on
his shirt and tie, unembarrassed.
He talks with us with good humor
over a ribbon greeting.
            As we often do, we go,
after seeing the mayor,
to the city employees' union, usually
an office in a basement, but for once here
it's upstairs in sunlight. On shelves I notice
five squat game tables, among them
the *shohgi* (chess) that Hashi played
at the Ube inn. The union
gives us a contribution
matching the mayor's. We go on to Mitoo,
and on the mayoral office wall
we see the picture of a man grim
and ready to split a body
with the great curved samurai sword
he carries under his left arm. Again
over green tea
we are welcomed and helped.
            We visit still another city,
Shin Nan Yo, where we meet
the President of the City Council.
He and his brother, he tells us,
were in the army, he posted in Korea,
his brother in Hiroshima.
His brother was killed by the A-bomb.
He survived. It used to be
those expecting to be killed
were at the fighting front. Today
cities are unsafe places.
            The President says
there are sixty-six *hibaksha*

in this small city.
"Every community has its victim count,"
he says. All Japan lives
with Hiroshima and Nagasaki.

July 27.   At Tokuyama Station

As the march arrives in late afternoon
at Tokuyama Station,
a man comes to Morioka
and gives him a plastic container
labeled SAN KYO LEOPIN CAPSULES,
filled with five hundred one-yen pieces.
The story behind his jar:
a couple living near the station,
the Nakatas, told their two daughters,
Mutsumi and Aya,
about the march that was coming,
that it was good, that it was for peace,
so the two girls
began to save one-yen pieces,
inserting them in a slot in the lid
of this empty medicine jar
until they had five hundred pieces,
about two dollars.
Now here these yen lie, a mass
of little aluminum coins. Morioka
holds them up. The marchers, moved,
come to see and touch the child gift,
an offering
beyond the collection boxes' or even
the mayors' gifts—an unasked gift.

July 27.   *Mino*

The American Mino de Angelis,
tall and quiet, wears his hair
in the current gathered ponytail
at the back of his head.
He can do rather good carpentering.
He finds the positive aspect
of some of the things Jim hates.
Religion. Mysticism.
But he is not what you would call
a believer in abstractions.
        He says
that over the winter of 1968/69
he and Hashi hitched from Amsterdam
across Europe and northern Africa
and went further east at last
to India and Nepal.
Hashi stayed in India for a year.
He had told Mino about the beauty
of his wife's sister.
Mino, returned, found her and married her.
Yo-chan is his stepdaughter, a fine
small laugher.

July 28.   *Incident with a Comb*

Yo-chan
has a comb
and is combing the young Buddhists' hair,
amusing them.
Morioka takes the comb from her and passes it
over his own clean-shaved head, saying,
"Does it look all right now?"

July 29.   Office Art

The art in mayors' offices: in Iwakuni
this afternoon, the print of a hand
placed in red paint, then on paper,
and ideograms written beside it
in black brush strokes. The compositional
attack of this picture is so good
it would not be out of place in a museum.
        Yo-chan,
sitting beside Morioka, says,
"Is that the Mayor's hand?"

July 29.   The Demonstration

We talked by loudspeaker
across the moat at the naval base
at Sasebo. Today,
twenty miles from Hiroshima,
we have our first demonstration.
Morioka, all the Americans,
the Buddhist young men with drums,
Yo-chan, Anna (Hashi's daughter), four of us
carrying extemporized posters
demonstrate for an hour
at the Marine Corps Air Station
in Kawashimo ward
of Iwakuni City.
A sign by the main gate says:
"Home of the First Marine Aircraft Wing
United States Facility and Area
U.S. Forces in Japan
Unauthorized Entry Punishable
by Japanese Law."
          As we begin our demonstration,
assembling on a road on the near side
of a moat (on the far side, the fenced base),
some marines clap in a friendly way,
standing in the doorway of a barracks.
We open our black and white posters:
"U.S. MILITARY, GO HOME"
"NO MORE HIROSHIMAS,
NO MORE NAGASAKIS"
"PEACE PRESENCE, NOT WAR PRESENTS"
The fourth poster, which I hold,
has on it the main march symbol,
a fist crushing the mushroom cloud.
More marines now appear
at the ends of the barracks building

and in windows. Jim Peck
takes the loudspeaker and says,
repeating our poster slogan,
"U.S. military, go home."
One marine calls back,
"We want to go home," and raises
a two-finger victory salute.
Jim: "We are Americans for peace.
We don't want atomic bombs.
No more Hiroshimas, no more Nagasakis."
"What about Pearl Harbor?" a marine yells.
Jim: "Atomic war anywhere, by any country,
is insanity." There are derisive cries
and a marine in a window shouts,
"Commies, go home." Our long line
of monks in robes, Quakers, advocates
of nonviolence face marineward
and smile. Yo-chan smiles and waves her hand.
We sing "We Shall Overcome"
and walk up and down in a circling line,
our posters flashing as the line turns.
Military Police now arrive
and begin dispersing the marines,
sending them away. At the same time
large silver-colored warplanes
rise one after another, their fumes darkening
the sky. Smaller planes with red on them
follow as if to show themselves too
to these few peace people.
          We learn later
that the main gate, open when we came,
was closed while we were there
and only reopened after we left.

166

July 29.   The Gun

As we leave,
we follow a military truck
that has a gun in tow,
its large barrel pointed to the rear
at us.

July 29.   *Hiroshima Prefecture*

At Otake City
we cross the Oze River,
a wide river, a wide bridge to walk over,
with new marchers
waiting at the other end. Hiroshima,
the final prefecture,
the final welcome. Our luggage is transferred
to the Hiroshima cars
with a drum-stroked ceremony,
and we feel
near the end.

July 29.   The Rebuilding

I ask when Hiroshima
was rebuilt. "Oh, it wasn't long."
As soon as the radiation
left the ground,
the devastation and char were cleaned away
obsessively
and the city was replanned, streets to be straightened,
widened, new trees planted along them.
The main railroad station was redesigned
as an inner-city shining train-port.
The city
"became beautiful again."

July 29.   Night Talk in Otake

We stay tonight in Otake
in a children's school. Natalie Shiras
of the AFSC
arrives to spend the night with us.
She has been on the main walk,
and there is a problem about Gensuikyo.
Some Americans have held meetings
instead of marching, troubled.
Gensuikyo says it is unbiased,
but some marchers feel/suspect
that Communist elements in it
are against only nonCommunist
armaments. And as for nuclear power,
Gensuikyo says it is
for complete nuclear disarmament
but doesn't want the issue
of "the peaceful use of nuclear energy"
to divide the antibomb movement,
and particularly in connection with that,
the report is that Gensuikyo is censoring
"freedom of expression."
        As we talk,
I remember Yanigihara
on the way to Matsuura, his happiness
at the march's unity.

170

July 29.   Natalie Sleeping

Tonight, preparing to sleep, I lay out
my sleeping bag and mattress
         (*futon* are in short supply)
on the floor of a groundfloor schoolroom
under an open window.
A Buddhist lights a coil of green
mosquito-repellent that will burn all night
and presumably keep mosquitoes away.
I close my eyes, I spread my body
uncovered in the heat
within the narrow space of my bed.
A whine in my ear.
Why do mosquitoes let you know
they are there (here)?
The first bite, the first slap,
and soon my ankles itching.
I keep moving them in vain.
I begin to scratch, delightful agony.
Marguerite Tirk, to my right,
in the darkness gets to her feet
and walks the floor.
I control myself and lie burning
(in more ways than one).
         On my left, Natalie Shiras
is peacefully sleeping.
I can hear her even breathing
and she does not move.
How is it possible?
After an entire night
of my own sleeplessness,
in the morning I discover that she is
wound in a nearly invisible
gauzy sheet of mosquito netting
from which she emerges
rested, refreshed.

July 30.   Kiyo Matsufuji

Kiyo-san gives me a sweatshirt
with the march insignia on it.
I am getting to know her.
She was born October twenty-first,
nineteen fifty-four. She is one
of seven children—three boys, four girls.
Her mother is her father's second wife,
the first wife having died in childbirth.
The first wife
had only boys. The second wife
had only girls.
Kiyo has a strong face
bearing a trace of tenacity
in its sweetness. She is now twenty-two.
After high school she attended
an architectural school in Osaka,
then worked as a draftswoman, drawing
in an architectural firm's office
and in city and prefectural offices.
She stopped work March tenth of this year.
The reason: "A TV camera"
was installed in the firm's workroom
"so the president could watch us."
It was more than she could bear.
She began to work then for peace.
"I think small peace
grow to big peace." She is now
with Gensuikyo, she is on
the Central Committee of the march,
but she is on the committee
"in name only. Peace is in the mind."
I believe I know what she means,
that committee work is secondary
to individual conviction.

July 30.   *Moriko Sasayama*

We go to see the mayor in Otake.
Waiting outside the town hall,
I talk with a woman employed there,
Moriko Sasayama.
She wears gray-checked pants
and a blue blouse with an embroidered symbol
like linked horns. She says,
"At the time of the Hiroshima bomb,
I had nine brothers.
One was at the hypocenter and was killed
and two others died."
Her remaining brothers were at Kobe
and escaped. Her husband
was not in Hiroshima in the morning
but came in the afternoon
because his own brother died
and he wanted to find the body.
So he was exposed to radiation.
"Now he's sometimes tired. He rests."
She quickly denies
that he goes to the hospital.
It is not that bad. He is careful
and can care for himself. That is all.
        Along the side of the town hall
a row of tree-like plants grows
called *yatsude*. The word means
"eight-fingered leaves," and the plant's leaves
do look like fingered hands,
hands held out, asking
compassion.

July 30.   "Scroll of Hells"

A marcher today has a postcard
"Edited by Tokyo National Museum,"
a detail of a painting, "Scroll of Hells,"
done seven hundred years ago
by Jigoku Zoshi. The painting shows
women and men lying on the ground, naked,
reddened by a peculiar exploding
rain of fire. Others
are floating in a river.
        In 1975 Tomoe Harada,
a nonprofessional painter, painted
a scene he remembered from the atomic
bombing of Hiroshima:
writhing bodies, red burns, corpses floating
in one of the delta rivers.
In both paintings the same screams
from wide-open, blackened mouths.
Even, in both paintings,
the buttocks of an upended body
in the water. What is unalike:
one is imagination,
the other real.

July 30. Shigemi Oka

On the last lap of the walk today,
at Hatsukaichi,
a cripple comes with us in a wheelchair,
Shigemi Oka.
He wheels himself along.
At the stopping point I get Kiyo-san
and Hozo, one of the young Buddhists,
to help me talk with him.
I ask them to ask him,
"Why are you walking with us?"
　　　He says, "For two reasons,
because thirty-two years ago
the atom bomb was dropped,
and because of the neutron bomb."
The neutron bomb
has just been announced as a proposal
by the United States; great indignation
in Japan, a bomb
that destroys people, not property.
So Oka is marching.
He has no shoes on. His down-curved
crippled feet are in socks.
　　　　"How did you get hurt?" I ask him.
　　　　"I was a soldier."
He rests in the sloping chair
and after a moment says, through Hozo,
"Now is peace in Japan,
but is not true peace. Only true peace
is no bomb."
He hopes that more people in America
will want peace.
"American people for peace
and Japanese people for peace are—"
now struggling for the word,

Hozo knits his hands to show me—
together. I say, "Are together."
He repeats it, "Are together."
Oka says something. Hozo says,
"And nothing will"—he makes a smashing motion
with his hands.
            "Break?"
            "Break this unity."
            Oka looks satisfied.
We shake hands and I thank him
for talking. He wheels himself away.

July 30.   *Entering Hiroshima*

1

From the stopping point of the day's walk,
the Buddhists, the Americans
are taken in cars to Hiroshima
to the Sangha temple and stupa
where we will sleep overnight.
We still have to come back tomorrow
and with another day's group
make a formal entry on foot.
        Now
we drive along a hill road, Route 2,
and come to a sign,
HIROSHIMA CITY LINE. Soon,
in the flat valley below
glimpsed in openings in the hills,
Hiroshima
clean and white, new,
many buildings with a curious
unstained, undiscolored look, a sweep
of modern metropolitan high-rise
magnificence. Openness.
Can it be believed that this open great
city was totally destroyed,
"everything down in the atomic blast (*pika*)
except a few cement buildings"?
And even these buildings badly damaged
and completely burnt out.
        Through the hills our four cars
descend into the city,
and now we can see, to the left, far up,
the Peace Pagoda, the stupa
above the Buddhist center,
a silver structure, round like a bell jar
and narrowing in thin recessions to the usual

pinnacle staff.
      We cross bridges over
branches of the Ota River, and drive
up through hill alleys to the "training center,"
the temple. On a terrace
past an outdoor shrine is a single
interconnected long building
with kitchen, monks' and nuns' quarters,
the temple itself,
and a large guests' sleeping room.
Monks and nuns come out to greet us,
bowing deeply.
      We bow.
      Morioka and his Buddhists,
having chanted at the shrine,
enter the temple and begin
a service of arrival. Many Americans
join.

2
After dinner Morioka
invites us to visit the stupa.
Under the coruscating stars
we climb three hundred steps to a hilltop,
a level space
on which the stupa is built, inset
with a dim seated Buddha.
Nothing inside the stupa,
no entry. It is there
just to say—
its silver hemisphere against the sky—
Peace.
      Beside it,
a railinged walk. The moon is up.
Morioka earlier had called to me—
"Millen," through a window—
to come and see the moon, a red disk

178

like an enlarged Mars with a red
nimbus around it, a moon color
I had never seen before,
a color of wrath and yet,
halfway up the night sky, the disk a flower,
red petals circling its center.
There it is, still rising,
and under it the city,
a lighted wheel of avenues
across which, gleaming,
the railroad track from Yaga Station
curves to the main Hiroshima Station.
As we watch,
a train comes in, a line of window lights
ending in a red tail-light like a period
to a traveling sentence.
          The hypocenter
of the bomb is to the right
about two miles away,
Peace Park and the deliberately kept
Dome whose stripped bare girders
and broken supporting walls
are what remains of the Industry
Promotion Hall. Hiroshima,
there it lies below us
restored, rebuilt, even resplendent,
beautiful with lights, but its people—
how must they carry within them,
consciously or unconsciously, the sense
of their dark centrality to the world.

July 30/31.   Night and Morning

Jim and I and others
sleep on the *tatami* floor in the guest room.
At five-thirty in the morning,
the big temple drum begins sounding,
morning service. Now follows chanting,
a service almost as loud
in our room as in the temple—more drums,
more voices, and the approaching light
of dawn. Impossible to sleep.
We stagger up
and go out on the morning terrace,
the balcony over the city,
and see mostly
mist.

July 31.   *Formal Entry*

Today most of the Americans
who came in with Jim and me last night
and the long-distance Buddhist marchers
are taken by car to yesterday's stopping point,
and with a new group
on foot, in a walk of several hours,
we officially enter Hiroshima.
We do not go
much beyond the city line, because
tomorrow we will be returning here
and marching the still long distance
into the center of the city
to Peace Park
to meet the main march there. Now
we are taken back by car to the temple.
        On the temple terrace
tents are being put up,
bright blue sides and orange tops,
extemporized pavilions
for the many from the main march
who tonight will overflow
every floor.

July 31.   Itaru

I'm sitting resting on the terrace.
Sumako Tamura comes to say hello.
She can speak English.
She has a gamin look
and depths and amusements.
She carries her ten-month son
Itaru. His name means
"reaching far, reaching up."
"I hope he reaches up far," she says.
        "He is big, strong."
            "I give him good milk. He is strong."
        I have had a glimpse of her
nursing him. In the guest room
he lies on the *tatami* matting
and she leans over, giving him her breast.
She says her husband Aki
is at "many meetings," arranging
a concert and festival
to be held on "the island," Ninoshima,
that island where so many suffered,
wild with thirst, dying.
        She asks if I know a Japanese
poet, Nanao, whom she and her husband
know. He is a friend
"of Gary Snyder. He has translated
Turtle Island. He also knows
Allen Ginsberg." Her small face
is still gamin-like but tender
towards Itaru, the reacher. He reaches
for her lips. Gently
she draws away his hand. "Nanao
writes his own poems
both Japanese and English.
He lives in Nagano

inside the mountains there,
a very quiet place."
　　　"Like Gary Snyder."
　　　She smiles and nods. Itaru
begins to fuss, so she goes away,
perhaps to give him more good milk.

July 31/August 1. *The Tokyo Marchers Arrive*

1

In the late afternoon
the permanent marchers from Tokyo
and the Americans who joined them near Osaka
arrive in four cars at the temple
as we did yesterday.
        I have told Sumako Tamura
that perhaps Yoshiko Miyano
will be with them, Yoshiko
whom I knew last year in New York
and in Washington. I watch the unloading
and now I see her
standing behind one of the cars,
heavy short black hair,
a bang low over her forehead,
and those familiar shoulders. So many thousand miles
and here she is again. She sees me
and waves. I go to her
and we stand cheek pressed to cheek,
arms around each other,
patting each other's backs.
She speaks to me in Japanese,
but knowing I cannot understand,
she asks me in English about my "health."
        "I'm all right."
        She draws her hand
over my chest, indicating
I am well. A demonstrativeness
uncommon in the Japanese.
It is Yoshiko, her way, or perhaps
that she has been in America.
But it is hard to talk
with almost no language.

184

When we have said what we can,
she asks after Jim Peck
and I show her Jim standing talking
and she and he greet each other.

2

Meals now are served on the terrace, on carpets
near large cooking kettles that rest
on stones over fires, steaming.
Dozens of cups, and bowls of stew.
And Jim and I sleep now in the temple.
It is so crowded
I cannot reach my legs full length
or I disturb a Buddhist. In the morning
again before dawn, the drums, and the Buddhists
rising. The new Americans stayed up late,
but experienced Jim and I
want to bed soon after twilight.
Some, desperate,
try to sleep again outside,
but monks come out and chant a service
at the corner shrine.

3

Again on a carpet
I sit by Yoshiko for breakfast.
She tells me
she slept above, at "the pagoda.
The mosquitoes, zoom." She zooms a finger
into her arm. How did I sleep?
        "I slept till three, then zoom,
mosquitoes." We eat,
our shoulders together against an old
cherry tree with bands of gray bark
that ants are running up like private
staircases. Around us

a dozen conversations hidden from me
by Japanese. *"Nanno . . . koshin . . . dame."*
The drums, the increasing heat,
the continued gray haze over the city,
and Mino de Angelis tells me
more about Nanao Sakaki, poet.
He is from an old Daimyo family.
He believes in Su-Wa-No-Se,
the fourth world, a world
where people live in myth, not even
in the third world, in a world apart
that includes animals, plants,
nonliving things. His name
for Japan in this world
is Japanesia.

August 1.   Yoshiko Miyano

After breakfast I talk more with Yoshiko
with her beginning English
and my nonJapanese.
She tells her birthday,
January 29, 1950.
"I'm old. Twenty-seven."
        "No, young."
        She shakes her head.
She went to high school in Arao, near Kumamoto,
and after graduation
went to nursing school for three years.
        I write for her,
"What made you do peace work?"
        She says, studying the sentence,
"I know the words but not put together."
        "Why peace work?"
        Now she understands.
"It was nineteen forty-five,
Hiroshima, Nagasaki,
and I must work." Work for peace.
        I assume she will go on working.
"What will you do next, after?"
        "I don't know,
don't know where I will be."
She would like to go to Sri Lanka
to help build the Peace Pagoda.
"I want to go to India."
Buddhism as Fujii is changing it
with what Morioka calls "power,"
the power of his spirit—that change
back to the beginning
attracts her. She will submit herself
to it. Its goal is affection. Love.
        Nearby

on the swept temple ground
shouts of amusement as the young men
and a small girl in a red dress
play a game of turning over cards.
"Wah. Hah." *"O-sama."*
The emphatic shout and laugh
as memory works or fails.
"Wah."

August 1.   The Shrine

The corner shrine
is a tall slab of granite with—
on its polished face,
like a continuous downward drawing—
the chant chanted so often
to the beating drums
for arrivals, departures,
for morning service, evening service:
"Namu myo ho ren ge kyo."
      I have never asked what it means
and ask Morioka now. He says
it is untranslatable,
is an essence, is itself alone. But also
it means peace, it means human goodness.
      On the terrace
as we talk,
two mourning doves stroll
under marigolds, doves
different, full-feathered and more dovelike
than ours. Their call too is different,
again more dovelike, more a soft,
hurried cooing. They are calling peace,
coo and the lower coo coo coo.

August 1.   Peace Park

Today
the main march and the Nagasaki march
are to meet at Peace Park.
In the Nagasaki march are Jim and I,
the Tottori group of Americans,
the Buddhists, and many local people
from the outskirts of Hiroshima.
We start from Itsukaichi Station
at one o'clock. For a long distance
there are half-country scenes,
rows of fig trees, rice fields—even
within the city limits, vacant lots
of rice; no overview of the city,
only the level closing-in of houses.
        Hiroshima, the flat city.
        At a rest stop
as I sit chewing a stick of ice
on a step, a girl comes and sits beside me,
Izumi Yamanouchi.
Her first name, Izumi, she tells me,
means "fountain." She says,
"I like Indian philosophy.
My mother
was hurt by the A-bomb.
She was sixteen and lived on the island
Ninoshima.
She went to school in Hiroshima
but was sick on August sixth
and stayed home. All her classmates
were killed. She was hurt but not badly.
She is still alive." The accident
of life or death that I come upon
often with *hibaksha*. The fountain girl
is about to tell me more,

but the line of march must start again
and I take my place beside Jim
just behind a Japan-sun Buddhist pennant
that blows around our heads.
        After two more rest stops
we cross the main Ota River,
and I think of how people
were particularly exposed on bridges
and burned and died.
        We reach Peace *(Heiwa)* Boulevard,
wide, with a central row of trees
and trees on either side.
They all have about the same height
and walkways go among them. Before long
we have a glimpse of the Dome's iron girders,
those peeled ribs,
and begin to come in sight
of Peace Park. As in Nagasaki
the space under the bomb's hypocenter
is now a park, bounded here
by two more branches of the Ota River.
Again two bridges
and memories of flame.
And now the plume of a fountain
and, behind it, architecturally severe,
the single floor of the Peace Museum
raised on rows of posts.
        But we are looking not at the Museum
but beyond, down the Boulevard,
at the line of marchers coming toward us,
arms raised, cheering. The exaltation of approach,
the moment—
after long days of crossing
two islands in the heat, the relentless heat—
of nearing, of at last merging
in the center of bombed
Hiroshima.
A disarray of emotion, of unchecked

feelings. The moment given
is brief. On
under the Museum, up steps
to a black metal arch
in the form of a symbolic saddle,
the Cenotaph,
under which lies a chest
containing the names of all the known
A-bomb dead.
      Loudly
Buddhist drums are beating.
The large temple drum
is rolling up on a small truck,
a monk beating it. The space
above the steps, in front of the Cenotaph,
fills and through it four Buddhists
carry the image of Buddha
fastened on a pillow on a rack
on their shoulders. Flowers are strewn,
there is chanting, prayer, voices calling
through the Cenotaph arch.
Below the arch platform, below the steps
under banners still blowing in the wind,
the marchers wait. The arch space is cleared,
and the Reverend Fujii,
venerable ninety-two-year old
Buddhist renovator, smiling,
is seated, guided by helping hands,
and begins to speak.
He has an old thin, high voice like a bird's
but strong. He talks long,
but I understand
that he asks for just one thing,
"Stop killing. This march
is to stop killing. End war."
      When he finishes,
a beautiful young woman, Fu Mizuta,
holding a bouquet of flowers,

tries to speak.
It is known that she will denounce
Gensuikyo, so
she is kept from the microphone,
and other speakers drown her out—
perhaps a mistake. Jim Peck
is called to give his speech.
He gives it and sings
"Genbakuo Yurusumaji,"
the song of the march. Afterward,
he looks around for somebody
to hand the microphone to,
and there is the girl. He hands it to her—
not intentionally, he says later—
and she takes it and gives her speech.
It is unhappy that at a peace ceremony
there should be controversy, but perhaps
the moment of nonpeace is absorbed,
made part of the larger longing of a people
to agree and come together.
            Kiyo-san speaks, her voice
firm and appealing in its cadences.
In the sky
the sun is setting, arrowy pink clouds
tinting the Dome, and behind us
the fountain is spraying upward,
a cooling backdrop. We listen
to the speeches and afterward
sit on the steps, not dispersing,
wanting still to be with one another,
to prolong our companionship.
Many will be staying in Hiroshima
till the sixth
for the bombing anniversary,
but this meeting at the Cenotaph,
            symbol and door
            holding the Dome in its arch,
is the real end of our march.

August 2.   The Museum

Jim and I walk down from the temple
to the Peace Museum. Its single floor,
unlike Nagasaki's
Atomic Bomb Material Center,
is carefully planned. A central pit
with a model of Hiroshima
after the bomb. Devastation
clear to the mountains. Everywhere except where
a low hill saved some houses.
Photographs of the leveled areas.
A life-size model of three victims
walking half-naked, reddened, with skin dripping
from their fingers. The expression
staring, stunned, a look of nonunderstanding,
a look saying,
"We do not know what it is."
Stone crumbled, wall copings raised
far from the hypocenter, women, girls
losing the pride of their hair, their heads
bowed. Burned tongues, burned jaws.
Eyes ruined, and as in Nagasaki
clocks stopped, here with the hands
at eight fifteen. The moment
when every ordinary motion
of work, of walking, raising a cup to the lips
ended.
        Near the exit a sign says in English,
"So that was how Hiroshima perished."

194

August 2.   Comment

The Museum has a guest book
for those leaving to sign.
Over a right-hand column
is a request for "Comment."
One comment written in this column:
"I am ashamed to be an American."
I point it out to Jim and say,
"If there was a museum
showing all the earth's
wars, persecution, torture,
genocide and tries at genocide,
and if it had a guest book there,
what would the comment be?"
    Jim says, "Yes, Millen,
but still we dropped the bomb."

August 2. *Walk in the Park*

Jim and I walk through Peace Park.
We pass the mound of unidentified dead
and various memorial boulders,
but what we really want to see
is the Children's Peace Monument.
We find it, a vaulted cone protecting
thousands of paper cranes
and, on top, the short-skirted girl
Sadako Sasaki
with upraised arms holding
the metal outline of the paper crane—
      the girl who wanted
      not to die.

August 2.   The Hiroshima House

1

At 652 Ujina Nishi
is a house with a large *tatami* room
looking out on Hiroshima Bay—its shutters
flickering with reflections from the water.
        The director of the house,
Koichiro Tanabe,
sits at a low table. His wife
sits beside him. Off in a group to themselves
are four quiet *hibaksha* women
whom Tanabe has arranged for me to talk with.
But first, the House:
        In 1952, seven years after the bombing,
two novelists, Edita and Ira Morris
(she a Swede, he an American),
were living in India and decided,
before returning to Europe,
to stop off in Japan, in Tokyo.
Hiroshima was an afterthought.
They flew there for a one-day visit
but stayed—a month. The first night
a leading Hiroshiman painter
to whom they had an introduction
fainted at dinner. Later the same evening
a young guest fell ill. The Morrises asked why.
"They suffer from radiation sickness."
The following day the Morrises
visited the Museum, then "a mere shack"
but filled with unspeakable horrors.
Mrs. Morris later told me:
"I am not a woman who weeps—
at least not about my own griefs—
but I spent our third night in Hiroshima
weeping on our balcony."

At dawn she woke her husband
and said they must "do something." He agreed.
"We had noticed that the citizens of Hiroshima
neither smiled nor laughed. I said,
'Let us help them smile a little.'"
They rented a "modest tea-house," and aided
by their Japanese daughter-in-law,
the ballet dancer Ayako Ogawa,
furnished "oh so modestly"
"Ikoi no Ie," "The House of Solace,"
as it was called in Japanese.
Koichiro Tanabe
was hired to be its director, a man
sympathetic and with a feeling
for *hibaksha.* Since then over ninety thousand
atom-bomb survivors
have paid a visit to the House,
enjoying the hot baths (the public baths
didn't want them with their unsightly scars),
light meals, movie shows, dances,
"and many other small joys."
Appeals for funds were later made,
Americans giving generously,
and many of the internationally famous
sponsored the house: John Hersey,
Jean-Paul Sartre, who came to visit,
Lord Boyd Orr, Albert Schweitzer,
Gunnar Myrdal: of the Japanese,
Yasunari Kawabata who wrote
Thousand Cranes, and Shinzo Hamai who later
became mayor of Hiroshima.
Many more.
Every year, in August,
the Japanese P.E.N. Club
holds an auction of contributed
"calligraphic works" by members
to help fund the House.

198

2

The *hibaksha* now
sit in a modest half-circle
gathered around me to talk.
I have an interpreter, Yoko Ano,
a dark-eyed young woman
who listens and tells what they say.
They are
Ikuko Yamada, forty-eight,
Sadako Azechi, seventy-six,
Yoshiko Mazaki, seventy-two,
and Ikuyo Ishikawa, eighty-two.
All have been married. The husbands of three,
victims of the bomb too, are dead.
Mrs. Yamada's husband only is living.
When the bomb fell,
she, a girl of sixteen, was on her way
to market, pushing a cart
with her mother. She went to the toilet,
she saw the flash, so she put her hands
over her face. "Mother was outside,
so her arms were burned. When I came out,
it was dark—" I interrupt.
Darkness in daytime? All the women
assure me it was dark "for five minutes."
And they mention "the black rain."
They are together
in that post-bomb experience.
Mrs. Yamada continues: "We went home.
There was no medicine at home
for Mother's arms. She thought there might be some
at the school, so we went there.
No medicine there. Meantime my aunt,
who lived next door to us,
had been on the Yanagi Bridge.
This was about a kilometer and a half
from the hypocenter, no protection,
so she was badly burned.

She died in four days.
My mother survived."
          Mrs. Azechi was two kilometers from the bomb.
She had just moved from a home
at "the center of the bomb,"
so her life was saved. Even so
she was hurt. The bomb blast
blew bits of glass in her face.
She fainted. When she recovered,
she found herself at the door,
blown there. It was dark.
Terrified, she and her husband,
like many others, went to the school.
All who were there had homes badly damaged
and unlivable, and the school
could not house them all.
The Azechis for four days
slept outside on a carpet on the grass,
then went to the country.
          "Did you have children?"
          "One son. He was in the army,
so he was unhurt." That irony.
          Mrs. Mazaki now speaks.
The day of the bomb, by chance,
she had gone from her Hiroshima home
thirty-five kilometers
into the country. She saw the *pika*
and then the mushroom cloud.
Because of "the flash," she thought the bomb was nearer
and had hit an electric plant.
Nobody knew what it was. She had a daughter.
The daughter, as it happened, was in the outskirts
of Hiroshima when the bomb fell,
and was unhurt,
but both daughter and mother
returned to their home to find each other,
to the now irradiated central part
of the city,

so both became victims.
      Mrs. Ishikawa
the morning of the bomb
went by train to Saijo
but returned in the evening,
so she too, by returning,
became a victim.
      These four women,
like the chorus of a Greek play
in this sun-and-water-tinted room,
tell me of hurt, though it was for them—
by pure accident—
less than that of others.
Those for whom it was worse
are in hospitals or have died.

August 4.　　The World Friendship
　　　　　　　　Center

1

Today the clouds
coast lightly in the early
afternoon sky, all morning mist
burned away. Jim and I
are down in Hiroshima to visit
Barbara Reynolds, an old friend of his, like him
an inveterate peace activist.
We approach a house that might be
a private home. It is not.
It is the World Friendship Center,
an unpublicized peace center
on a side street. It has
the usual Japanese low portico
and sliding doors, *shoji*.
　　　　Barbara opens the front door
and greets Jim fondly,
and I'm introduced to her, glad at last
to meet a woman I've heard much about.
She founded this Center
with a Japanese surgeon,
Dr. Tomin Harada,
in the early sixties, a place
where "internationals" of every nation
could come, stay, rest, and think
in the context of Hiroshima.
Think peace. It has sponsored
three world youth peace seminars,
and its program includes
constant peace education.
　　　　When the Center was opened,
Barbara for a while was its Director,
but she is back now in the States,

in Wilmington, Ohio, but from there
keeps in close touch
with the work here. She is here now
for the August sixth ceremonies.
She introduces us
to the Center's current Director,
Maurine Parker
from the Friends Yearly Meeting
in Philadelphia, Maurine a warm,
concerned Quaker, and we all go
to a room with a low table
and have green tea that Barbara
prepares. Jim mentions Honolulu,
and he and Barbara
recall that time:
After Jim's sailing in the *Golden Rule,*
Barbara and her husband Earle
tried to sail their own ketch, the *Phoenix,*
into the A-bomb-testing area.
They too were stopped and Earle
was arrested. Still,
the *Phoenix*
      like the fire-arising
      legendary bird
and the *Golden Rule*
caught the world's imagination,
individuals putting themselves
as bodies voluntarily
under the bomb, to stop the bomb.
      As to Barbara's present
activity, she has in Wilmington
an important research library
on the two A-bombings,
and she has been largely instrumental—
this is of great interest to me—
in having the children's book,
"In the Sky Over Nagasaki,"
translated into English, the book

the head of the Teachers Union
showed me in Nagasaki.
 Barbara says, "Quakers have helped us,
and we've been helped
by the Pennsylvania German
plain sects. We have a man coming
just graduated from the Mennonite
Biblical Center in Elkhart, Indiana.
He'll spend a year in Tokyo
learning Japanese
and then work here three years.
The Mennonites will completely
underwrite his expenses."
 "That's like the Mennonites," I say.
 "We also had Eva Harshbarger, a Mennonite,
here for a year, and we had a woman
from the Brethren, Leona Row."
 These names ring in me
like bells. I could be listening
on Crow Hill, beside the fields there.

August 4.   *The Trees*

The trees of Hiroshima
puzzle me. In a post-bombing photograph
I've seen one still standing
near the hypocenter. A Hiroshiman
explains it. "The blast *(don)*
was straight down. The trees right under
stayed, though with leaves stripped off.
Those at a distance,
were knocked over. Some smokestacks
right under the blast stayed. Some."
     I'm told another story. After the bombing
a certain tree was found standing,
though badly burned. People put crutches
under its limbs and wrapped it with rags
meant to replace the bark. They wanted
that tree so much, like them, to survive.

August 4.   A Marcher's Speech

A speech is made at a Hiroshiman
international peace meeting
by Nanci Lee Mon, an American.
It begins:
"I, with many other human beings
of diverse backgrounds,
have walked on the Tokyo-to-Hiroshima
Peace March, the *Heiwa koshin.*
We are all simple people
concerned with the world's future life.
We are not members
of a political party or sect,
but are speaking as individuals
to other individuals for peace.
In our objection to our violent world,
we came here
to walk and share and form
an alternative social group
attempting to live in peace.
We concern ourselves only
with that which peaceful folk need for life.
We gather food, cook, wash,
and mend our clothing. We teach each other
English and Japanese—
and when language fails, we share music.
We daily wipe each other's sweat
as the sun pours down . . . "

August 5.   The Parade

This morning we Americans
are to march with the Japanese
in a parade from Peace Park
to Kenritsu Taikukan,
the Gymnasium, for the opening session
of the '77 Unified World Conference
against A and H Bombs.
        Not just Hiroshimans
but thousands of delegates from cities and towns
all over Japan
wait in the Park, forming in line.
Many have ideograms
on their jackets. I ask
what the characters on a streamer say:
"Atomic fission
is still a remediable error."
        Among the Americans, some newcomers:
Ed Hedeman who initiated
the American Continental Walk;
a Sioux Indian, Lehman L. Brightman;
Harold Rickard and his wife, members
of the Fellowship of Reconciliation. At last
the parade moves.
        Something new:
we reach a business district
and on the far side of the street,
police.
I think, it may be for something else,
but no,
on our side of the street,
a still larger group, holding full-length shields
curved, glittering, side edge meeting side edge,
and eyes looking over the shields.
I'm told that violence-oriented groups

have threatened the conference.
"We did not ask police protection,
but they have come."
            We reach the Gymnasium,
a large building surrounded
by cindered ground and grass, and Jim and I
enter. Two long banks of benches,
steep-pitched, on either side
of a bare floor. We take seats
on the right-hand side, and the floor
begins to fill. Morioka
sits cross-legged toward the center,
and near him, Yoshiko and Kiyo-san.
Jim sees friend Sera
who walked with him from New Orleans.
When all is quiet, the Gymnasium packed,
speeches begin. They are good,
Peggy Duff (British, a great activist),
an Australian, women and men
from many nations. We hear the speeches
translated in plugs we put in our ears,
the voice of the world, and yet nothing
we hear moves us as much
as Nanci Lee Mon's quiet speech
that she wrote with several other young women:
"We daily wipe each other's sweat
as the sun pours down . . . "

August 5.   Pre-Departure

Tomorrow morning
is the anniversary of the bombing,
the city-wide gathering at Peace Park,
the thirty-second anniversary.
Jim and I will go together,
walking down from the temple.
          And tomorrow
Fujii Guruji
will be ninety-three years old and will have
an evening dinner in his honor.
          And Sunday the seventh,
Jim is taking a through train to Tokyo
while I take a night train to Osaka.
That same night
Morioka and others (some Americans)
will take a midnight train to Nagasaki
for the Nagasaki Conference there
on the eighth and ninth.
          This evening is clear and starry,
no mist, no flame-colored moon.
City lights below our temple terrace
are like a reflection of the stars.
The terrace is dark.
The cooking fires are out.
In preparation for departure
great piles of luggage everywhere,
backpacks and sacks, and laundry drying.
On the cluttered terrace
a crowd of young Buddhists and women
are gathered,
their eyes taking leave, winking,
themselves like stars.

August 6.   The Anniversary

1

Today is the official
ceremony at the Park. The Park
is filled with seats. Yesterday
workmen were swinging sledge hammers,
pounding barriers of fresh posts
into the ground. Today
these barriers are unnoticed
as arriving thousands fill the seats
and overflow. The sides of the park
are twenty-thirty deep—more—
with not only women and men
but children. Massed Boy Scouts wait
in the room of air under the Museum.
        At eight o'clock
a prayer, and the standing bow.
Even those still coming in
behind the Museum bow. Many now,
unable to get near, turn back. Overflow-fathers
lift children to their shoulders. Tired
children sit on steps lost
among legs, listening
and waiting. Speeches in Japanese.
Mayor Yoshitake Morotani
from Nagasaki is here,
Kurt Waldheim is here, from the United Nations,
many *hibaksha* are here, "explosion-affected"
women and men still living.
At eight-fifteen,
the exact moment of the bombing,
a thousand doves are loosed
and spiral in a fast, rustling movement
into the sky.
The TV cameras follow them up.

2

Beyond the Museum fountain,
on a curved approach to the Park,
a group of political extremists
is marching. Red banners
flap above them. They punch fists
rhythmically into the air
and shout. Many wear symbolic white
gags hiding their faces. Police
shoulder-to-shoulder
with another fence of shields
block them—more police than marchers.
As the demonstration swerves, forced away,
I find a young man who speaks English.
I ask him what the protesters are yelling.
        "That the official ceremony
is capitalist," he says.
"They are protesting exploitation."
        I thank him. The cries of anger die away.
Those remaining now are only
those who have come here to express
a city-felt grief and horror,
those who want
no further horror, no greater
secret instrumentation
against life, against their ordinary
hope to keep on living day-to-day.
No more Hiroshimas.
No more Nagasakis.
        No more death.
        Peace.

August 6.   The Birthday Party

Tonight
the Reverend Fujii
attends his ninety-third birthday party.
He walks well. His eyes are sharp with the charge he brings
of nonviolent action for peace.
        Among the guests who will speak
is Ichiro Moritaki, seventy-seven,
retired professor of ethics
at Hiroshima University.
He is a *hibaksha*. He was severely hurt
and lost an eye in the bombing.
He saw many friends and relatives die
and still feels them near him,
the dying and dead.
When, somewhere in the world,
an atomic bomb is tested,
he holds a personal vigil,
sitting cross-legged on the low steps
before the Cenotaph in Peace Park,
his head of silver hair bowed.
A little girl once asked him,
"Can you stop it by sitting?"
He does not say he can,
but he likens his sitting
to the will of a small child
balking parental authority.
Something may come of his vigil.
The Japanese, some say,
have reacted too much to the bomb,
but he says their reaction is healthy.
It is "nuclear insensitivity"
that is dangerous, is inappropriate
to humanity in the face of death.
        The Reverend Fujii

himself talks hard and long
to his guests to bring attention again
to the single necessity, "Peace,
which must come."

August 7.   *Jim Before He Takes the Train*

With his incredibly light luggage, a bag
slung over his shoulder, Jim stands
at the terrace side
among sword-edge plants, sabers of green,
Hiroshima under him. He tells me,
"It was good to make the march with you.
It would have been so easy to have somebody
who'd break your balls."
I laugh. Jim himself no ball-breaker,
but one who was steadily
helpful and enduring.
I remember a day
when a second contingent of marchers
kept us walking till eight o'clock at night
and Jim with his ulcer hurting. He said, then,
"If I fall out by the road,
it's a good ending."
        But now he wants to get home.
Get to Tokyo, get a plane, get home.
No urge
to see Japan nonmarching.
Walk in mountain-backed gardens
designed four hundred years ago,
see Osaka, Kyoto. No,
nothing can hold him. Get home.
He says goodby to Morioka,
thanking him for his many
kindnesses. Then
down the green bush-bordered road, and from below
he waves back.
"See you."

August 7.   Morioka Before He Takes
the Train

It is nearing midnight.
"I don't have good English to explain,"
but he talks with an infectious effort
that sends meaning through hints, through half-words,
through the movements of eye or arm.
He is telling me
how he became a monk. At first
he resisted the drum. He beat it lightly.
"I stood away" at the edge of the group
drumming, away from the heavy drum.
Drumming
produced dreams. He touches his head.
"Not always good dreams," but the beat
on his mind cleansed him—
he dreamed expiation. His father died,
and returned to him in dreams.
Not clear to me what his father meant to him,
but in the monotony, the loudening
of the drum he had him back.
He has three brothers and three sisters,
in some way delegates for children.
        At the temple earlier tonight
a woman laid her baby to sleep
on a mattress on the floor. She saw me lying
on the bare floor. She moved me
to the mattress beside her baby
and put a pillow to my head
and threw a cover over me.
As soon as I was beside the baby,
it quieted and slept. I slept.
What is this communication of presence,
warmth, pressure, a pulse that says,
I am here. The parent present.

In the drum did Morioka
find his father beside him?
        "Twice a year I fast for eight days."
He begins the first of the month
and fasts through the eighth. "The sixth day—"
He touches his stomach. "Hungry."
But he continues to the end.
"Then I am clean." In his face
the excellent cleanness, the renewal,
the renovation of the spirit.
"If a person has much money,
he changes." Not to want money,
to eat what costs little, to be concerned
for life. Buddhism.
This came to him in India.
He was mountain-climbing in Nepal.
He was a porter, in charge of porters—
some obsession in the snow
back from Katmandu. He heard
of Fujii, of Japanese Buddhists
who were starting to build a stupa
at Rajgir. He went there.
He speaks now of a "guru," not Fujii
but Tensho Yagi, an inimitable
small man who does not proselytize
but is "warm." Wears
a lopsided small
yellow turban.
"He saved my life. He told me,
'You will fall, useless.'" When two Sherpas fell
just ahead of Morioka,
he returned to the stupa.
From Rajgir to Sri Lanka.
        At Sri Pade
he is working. He breaks stone.
His paler skin deepens into the tone
of Sri Lanka laborers'. He carries in his arms
material for

216

the dedicated hemisphere
so rushing upward.
There is light as dawn
comes up on the mountains. On snow
or on remembered snow.
"You can see eight peaks."
There is a temple there and below it,
a lake. He uses the word "natural,"
that Sri Lanka is a place where man
can live with himself, supported
by accessible wonders. Light on the mountains,
shade on the lake
in the morning darkness. The drums
are calling to the heights.
" . . . ren ge kyo." His speech
is like the mantra,
an ennobling lack of words,
a self-giving passion
that smiles as he leaves me
in the long Hiroshima Station and goes
to take the train to Nagasaki.

August 7.   The Voice

Shin Higuchi later tells me
that small Yagi's voice when he chanted
was equal to ten men's voices
put together.

August 7.   The Lanterns

In Hiroshima last night, Jim and I
after Fujii's party
walked to the Motoyasu River
to see the hundreds of candle-lit lanterns
floating in a water-reflected line
downstream. From the bank near us
women and men, even children,
were reverently launching still more lanterns
on little rafts that moved out
into the procession of light, lanterns
"offered on the water
for the peaceful rest of the spirit."
        In a lake in New York's Central Park
I and others had once launched similar lanterns
for peace. The rafts here,
quivering under the arc of the Dome
in their almost unbearable beauty,
were for those who had suffered
the world's first A-bomb
agony and death.
        Near us
a woman stood with bowed head.
A child watched, silent.
A man put his hand over his eyes.
Thousands on both sides of the river
were silent too as if waiting
for some recognition,
some word of this moving line of light out
to the world, some word
heard.

Author's Note

Volunteer interpreters were steadily and generously provided for us and were indispensable for our full participation in the march. They were usually English teachers or students who could read and write English well, but most, as Yuko Tomita mentioned, had had little practice with spoken English. We had to go slowly, reaching for alternate expressions or the dictionary, and when I came to writing what was said, I had to consider whether or not usually to show this difficulty. I decided not to. Actually the slowness may have made the written dialogue more accurate, for I could take notes and dialogue stayed in my mind. When I sent copies of journal entries to many of those with whom we talked, without exception they said that what I had written was correct.

The entire book was gone over, most helpfully, by the Reverend Gyotsu Sato (who was close to the march), to check for factual accuracy. If any errors remain, they are not his fault.

I decided to shorten the word *hibakusha* to *hibaksha*, which is what it sounds like ordinarily. It has careful legal definitions, but in general it means a bomb-affected person.

It may not be out of place to mention that the poetic journal is an old and popular literary form in Japan.

Some acknowledgments:

Jim was of great assistance in sharing memories with me and suggesting poems, and to help me, he kept an itinerary of where we were each day.

The quotation from Tu Fu, recurrent in the book, is adapted from William Hung's translation in his biography of that poet.

The several mentions of Miyazawa and his liking for blue refer to the modern Japanese poet Kenji Miyazawa, who can be read in English in *Spring & Asura,* translated by Hiroaki Sato.

For background on the tea ceremony in "July 12. At the

Hiranos" I drew on Fosco Maraini's *Meeting with Japan,* also on Yasunari Kawabata's *Thousand Cranes.*

"August 6. The Birthday Party" is based on my meeting with Professor Moritaki and on information about him in an article in *The New York Times* for June 18, 1975, by Robert Jay Lifton, author of the important Hiroshima study, *Death in Life.*

My awareness of Japanese character, particularly in its relation to war, was deepened by Ivan Morris's book, *The Nobility of Failure.*

The Reverend Fjuii's autobiography, *My Nonviolence,* was useful but suffers from being only a partial translation.

My editor son Jonathan was invaluably perceptive and careful with me. Edward Field and Hayden Carruth read the manuscript and made detailed and important suggestions. My nephew John read me and helped. The Canadian poet Andrew Suknaski suggested a poem. My debt to them is as a writer, but Jim and I owe a personal debt to the Japan Buddha Sangha, our host, and to all the Japanese who aided and cooperated with us, particularly our interpreters.